The Definitive Answer
to the Meaning *of* Life

The Definitive Answer
to the Meaning *of* Life

JACK ABAZA

RESOURCE *Publications* · Eugene, Oregon

THE DEFINITIVE ANSWER TO THE MEANING OF LIFE

Resource Publications
An Imprint of Wipf and Stock Publishers
199 W. 8th Ave., Suite 3
Eugene, OR 97401

www.wipfandstock.com

PAPERBACK ISBN: 979-8-3852-0170-9
HARDCOVER ISBN: 979-8-3852-0171-6
EBOOK ISBN: 979-8-3852-0172-3
VERSION NUMBER 11/13/23

Veritas non habet domin

Contents

Preface

THIS BOOK WAS NECESSITATED by philosophy professoriates, intelligentsia, and masses of layfolk alike, who *overwhelmingly insist* that the meaning of life either cannot be solved or, if solvable, cannot be known for certain. After all, one would be hypocritical in ruling out the definitive answer to the meaning of life without evidence or deductive reasoning proving it so while relaxing the burden of proof on beliefs that conform to one's own.

Like a pendulum whose bob had swung too far to one extreme, the rebalancing event that immediately follows is the bob's swing to its other end, with similar force. I drive this rebalancing force, and the previous outcome decided between contrasting beliefs and wills is now the momentum that determines how far the bob pivots next. However, one would be mistaken in saying that the complete restoration of balance is when the bob stills, since a position of complete neutrality in philosophy is only attainable when nothing is said. For it is as Elbert Hubbard wrote, "[D]o nothing, say nothing, and be nothing—court obscurity, for only in oblivion does safety lie";[1] philosophy enigmatically involves many things, but silencing controversial claims—no matter how outlandish—is not one among them. With the latter kind of claim in mind, I am about to solve the meaning of life once and for all.

Had it not been for nihilists, relativism-inclined naysayers, problem-worshiping skeptics, and the general lack of academic seriousness that brought the philosophy of life to its knees, I would have never followed through with my book. But I must not forget

---

1. Hubbard, *Little Journeys*, 370.

theist philosophers' miscellaneous contributions to my inspiration, whenever they exclude from meaningfulness in their theories the lives of those who do not believe in their favorite religion. And then there are, of course, the objectivists, who proclaim few lives meaningful among the many, but only insofar as the living individuals concerned partake in accomplishments and activities deemed "worthwhile." I would have found these arbitrary exclusions amusing, if not for how sincerely authors believed in what they wrote and how unworthy of the meaning of life they believed anyone with differing opinions to be.

So, with renewed vigor, I took it upon myself—no matter how long its inquiry takes—to solve philosophy's greatest problem if it indeed has an answer.[2]

The theory of life herein presented is intended for those who—out of intellectual curiosity, rather than confirming bias—genuinely seek the answer that solves the meaning of life once and for all. But with more urgency, I likewise dedicate it to those who—like me—lost their way in life and are in desperate need of knowing *the* meaning of life. Most importantly, I intend an answer so robust that no skeptic, relativist, or nihilist—however mightily he attempts—could ever again sow the seeds of doubt and despair into the minds of his listeners; for the truth and certainty of my answer shall leave naysayers empty-handed when the time for their next harvest calls upon them to prey on peoples' hopes.

But I must caution that the answer herein does not confirm any of the preexisting beliefs I have encountered throughout my academic experiences or one with the purpose of encouraging human vanity. For a humbling anecdote, a younger, more naïve

---

2. The idea of writing journals was a suggestion from the professor who taught me in a course on the meaning of life. It is worth mentioning that the course itself was dissatisfying because it explored themes unrelated to the meaning of life (similar to Adams' anecdotes I quoted in chapter 2). I instead opted to write an essay initially and realized I could not consolidate half a million words of notes into roughly thirty pages or less. So, the professor's half-hearted suggestion eventually took a life of its own and materialized as a book, which I then downsized for a more focused delivery; it materialized into this book.

version of me began what eventually became a long, arduous journey on the path to solving the meaning of life; I began with the expectation that its inquiry would be quick and as easy as picking my favorite belief and rigorously defending it with whatever well-trodden arguments that pass for "eloquent" and "plausible" among philosophers. But as one attempt became a few and the few became many and eventually hundreds and then thousands, I balked despairingly and so much so that I had abandoned all hope and retraced my steps; by then, I had rewritten some individual chapters as many as 300 times, with the last complete rewrite of chapter 3 requiring me six months.

Realizing the truer picture of inquiring about the meaning of life had not only eluded me, but it also escaped the notice of many, as it is one seldom attained by even the most experienced and committed academicians; it is a path with not one, two, three—or a hundred—but perhaps ten thousand detours, including many backtracks and interludes. On its road are the thoughts oscillating between shameless confidence and complete disarray and despair, until, alas, the walk is over, and its destination is hardly any consolation for the mind-bogglingly maddening labor. Were my younger self less stubborn, and, thus, more relenting, and, most of all, more informed of the journey lying ahead, he would have given up for good. Still, my stubbornness had proved unusually opportune, and with my insatiable curiosity for knowledge, I could not forever ignore the calling to finish what I had started.

After much reflection, I learned to curb my expectations. However, my lesson was one learned the hard way, since the meaning of life had defiantly rebuffed all of my previous beliefs about it, until, alas, I reluctantly began to abandon them. Following René Descartes' lead, then, I re-examined my beliefs one after the other, until I rejected the teachings of my alma mater altogether, save for the forms of knowledge rightly considered indubitable; from there, I sought the theory that possesses the distinctive characteristics of science, mathematics, and logic combined, such as being neutral, transparent, meaningful, relevant, non-elitist, and somehow . . . tangible.

Over and above being already a decent writer, I relearned English fundamentals and mastered the writing skills necessary and set out to build a new theory for the third time. Armed with a method forged over the course of thousands of hours, spanning nearly a decade, I now confront the meaning of life anew.

J.A.

Toronto

August 27, 2023

My Writing Style

I URGE MY READERS to read this portion slowly and carefully, as this sets the style of writing for my entire book.

At the expense of clarity, readers may skip ahead to chapter I if they must. But the purpose of the explanations below is to make clear to readers when I am or am not referring to the strict meaning of words, ideas, and analyzable statements. Since I shall be making a *preponderance* of references to the strict meanings of words, ideas, and analyzable statements throughout this book, it is therefore easier for me to use quotation marks in non-standard ways.

Whenever I use single quotations around a word, phrase, or proposition, e.g., 'bachelor,' I am referencing either a word's strict, literal meaning, a concept, an analytic truth, or an empirical proposition.

If I quote an analytic proposition *that references a word*, I shall enclose the word thereof with a pair of single quotations, e.g., 'a 'bachelor' is an unmarried man.'

If I am referring to a word within any quoted phrase or proposition—enclosed in either single, or double quotations—I shall use double quotations, e.g., "meaning" in 'the meaning of life.' For example, if I write,

> The meaning of "meaning" in 'the meaning of life' is nuanced.

I am referencing the usage (i.e., the 'meaning' denoted) of the word "meaning" within the phrase 'the meaning of life.' Does the reader notice the word "in" in the above example? This is my way of making clear that I am referring to the word *exactly as it is used within a quote*. If I quote John Smith as having written, "The cat is on the mat" (123), I may further write,

> By "cat," Smith is referring to his neighbor's pet.

In this last example, it should not be construed that I am using scare quotes; I am clarifying Smith's particular *use* of "cat," but I am not referencing the *usage* of 'cat' as we saw with "meaning" in the example preceding the one concerning John Smith.

I may occasionally quote or basically repeat some of my previous material in this book for the purpose of clarity; if I do so, I shall often use double quotations, for example,

> In chapter 1, I mentioned that "I aim to solve the meaning of life in the English language *indisputably*."

The reader must remember my idiosyncratic uses of quotations.

The superscripts, which indicate footnotes, may provide useful information and may even answer questions that occur to readers. Therefore, the footnotes, usually appearing on the same page as their superscripts, should be read sooner rather than later.

Last of all, I use a comma to separate two authors of two separate papers; if the reader sees a comma between two or more authors, then I am indicating separate works.

Chapter 1

Discourse on Method

I AIM TO SOLVE the meaning of life in the English language *indisputably*; to be clear, I intend to provide an answer so precise that its truth is rendered unquestionable, yet, nothing short of revelatory about 'the meaning of life' verbatim. Since the meaning of life is a philosophical problem of such grand and self-evident importance, I need not waste any time emphasizing why it must be solved.

I

ABSOLUTES

Sound arguments are typically believed to be the best method of argumentation. But this belief is partly misguided because most sound arguments are not indisputable and could be called into doubt. If the "plausibility" of a deductive argument's premises is relative from philosopher to philosopher, then it is effectively pointless for one to try answering the question about the meaning of life; a skeptic only needs a crucial proposition within a valid argument to have a *single* possibility of being false in order to undermine its conclusion's truth-certainty. The resulting uncertainty leaves us with deceptively informative assertions that are closely accompanied with words like 'seems,' 'possibly,' 'perhaps,' or the phrase 'if I am not mistaken.' This is to say, dubitable assertions in philosophy are effectively as useless as silence. However, there is a way, other than distancing-language, by which academicians conceal the weaknesses of their claims; they may exaggerate the certainty of their claims with closely accompanied words such as 'surely,' 'certainly,' 'obviously,' or move from 'I' to the nosism 'we,' etc., as philosophers often do. In either case, an answer that is truly dubitable could never be asserted without the rebuttal "but how can you be sure?"

One needs to look no further than the writings of John Cottingham, and Julian Baggini to find a profligate abuse of duplicitous and non-committal language and references to poetry, movies, and anecdotes; they lack academic seriousness. Both authors reference Douglas Adams' comic novel, *The Hitchhiker's Guide to the Galaxy*. But the latter sets the bar to an embarrassing new low by quoting *Monty Python*—a television series known for its satirical parodies—for insight on one of philosophy's greatest problems. As the authors of two of the most influential *academic* books of the twenty-first century in the subdiscipline, Cottingham, and Baggini represent some of the "best" the philosophy of life currently has to offer. If anything useful shall ever be written in this area of study, it requires the type of answer that is completely independent of unjustified, unsubstantiated, or unfounded assumptions; this way, the answer to the meaning of life cannot be called into question and cast aside.

For an answer to be indisputable, it must not only possess the greatest argumentative strength, but it must also lack any possibility of being false. Absolute certainty is a step beyond "sound" argumentation and occurs whenever an argument is valid and *apodictically* true; it is indubitable and not merely so in virtue of philosophers acknowledging its premises' truths. In other words, it would be impossible for an absolute, sound argument's premises to be false under any circumstance, including philosophers' opinions, which are infamously indecisive, enigmatic, disingenuous, unforthcoming, volatile, and often hypocritical. Let us consider the following examples of declarative sentences with respect to 'the meaning of life':

"the" makes a definite reference;

"meaning" is singular, and

if "life" in 'the meaning of life' denotes a living thing, then carcasses and inanimate objects cannot have the "meaning" thereof.

As the aforesaid tautological propositions show, absolute certainty is attainable by deriving analytic truths strictly from what 'the meaning of life' denotes and nothing more. These analytic truths help discern which answer qualifies as relevant from those that are irrelevant to the discussion of the meaning of life and its solution.

I shall later elaborate on the first two propositions in this chapter, as well as the forthcoming chapters. However, the third proposition is controversial because 'life' has multiple meanings and serves only certain contexts, which is why the conditional 'if … then … ' is necessary.[1] Although I indeed critique Cottingham's uses of 'life' vis-à-vis 'the meaning of life' in chapter 2, I address the issue of ambiguity fully in chapter 6.

II

EMPIRICAL VERSUS ANALYTIC CLAIMS

Between epistemological impossibility, improbability, even-probability, high-probability, and absoluteness, the latter is, by definition, the best and only kind of truth-certainty for constructing apodictically true arguments. My aforementioned goal, then, necessarily requires the methical use of these indubitably true premises or tautologies; this way, their denials result in impossibilities, and the truth of my answer, being the conclusion following this kind of premise in a valid argument, would likewise be unquestionably true.[2] I shall thus forgo the use of empirical propositions in my final answer to the meaning of life, since they are dubitable

1. See *Concise Oxford Dictionary*, 10th ed. (1999), s.v. "life."

2. To keep this book readable within reason, the reader may rest assured that I shall omit to present my arguments in formal logic.

and form tenuous theoretical foundations. For even the slightest possibility that future empirical theories could eventually replace today's powerful, empirical theories leaves skeptics just enough room to cast doubt on their truth-certainties; this is an aspect of the infamous *problem of induction*. For example, the empirical proposition 'if the streets are wet, then it is raining' is dubitable on the basis of rain not being the only cause for streets becoming wet.[3]

Likewise, it is the case that not all causal factors are known of the most powerful, observation-based theories, such as evolution and physics; this may seem nauseatingly obvious in hindsight, but the possibility of missing, unknown factors tends to be taken for granted and ignored until a highly respected and popular theory is refuted or extensively revised.

Unless one is omniscient, like Laplace's demon, we can never be sure just how robust an empirical theory truly is. For several centuries, Newtonian physics was believed sturdy then as Einstein's theory of special relativity is today. The Newtonian equation ('F = ma') predicted earthly phenomena quite accurately and still does to this day. But that Newtonian equation thereof proved inadequate for predicting the curvature of light around large, celestial bodies like the Sun, in the way Einsteinian relativity ('E = mc2') does. But let us disregard unknown factors for the sake of argument and return to my earlier example.

Even if the only explanation for a street's wetness is rain, a skeptic with similar inclinations as those of Descartes, Berkeley, or Hume may still question whether its observation was imagined, dreamed, fabricated, mistaken, or hallucinated. If I may put it plainly: empirical propositions are the backbone of the physical sciences, but they are a nightmare to justify in a philosophy full of "reluctant" skeptics with questionable academic motivations. However, to be sure the meaning of life is not an empirical problem, I shall expound on the differences between physical and abstract sciences, including empirical and analytic propositions in the forthcoming chapters. By the last chapter, it should become

---

3. There is also the slight possibility that some of the streets in question are underground and completely sheltered from rainfall.

quite evident that, even if I sincerely tried to devise an empirical theory of the meaning of life, it would be impossible; if I were to force 'the meaning of life' into an empirical framework anyway, including the use of a person's life experiences—and anything observation-based—its answer would then acquire an indeterminate truth-value.

Contrary to the dubitability of empirical propositions, analytic statements, such as 'a 'bachelor' is an unmarried man,' cannot fail to be true; that is, if its context unequivocally entails the aforementioned homonym of 'bachelor,' as opposed to a 'bachelor pad,' for example. Should a theory of life be constructed properly, a skeptic who competently understands how truth-values work would know he has no legitimate epistemic and logical grounds to doubt its absolute truth.[4]

So, it is the propositions of the analytic kind I firmly have in mind for solving the meaning of life, and I shall elaborate on their tautological usages throughout this book. But, make no mistake, reiterations or regurgitations of the same bits of information in different words or different syntactical arrangements sometimes reveal new insights—even while no new information is produced from tautologies. I shall gradually elaborate on what these "insights" are and what they do in the following paragraphs, as well as throughout this book.

III

HOW TO SOLVE THE MEANING OF LIFE

Consider the semasiological tautology mentioned near the beginning: 'the "meaning" in 'the meaning of life' is *singular.*' Virtually every person whose first language is English would know of its truth because such a basic understanding of semantics is indispensable to *communicating intelligibly*; I discuss this point further in chapters 4–5. If a high-school dropout desires exactly one

---

4. But I am certainly unbothered by my adversaries disliking or feeling unhappy with my theory of life.

coffee, for example, they shall order a "coffee" and not "coffees." To an ordinary mind, the singular-plural distinction is insultingly platitudinal. But formal English tautologies, such as semantic and grammar rules, nevertheless serve in limiting the tendencies of those who ought to know better than to stray from the original question of an inquiry; if such a propensity is not prevented, philosophers would eventually stumble upon different, unrelated issues, e.g., claiming the meaning of life is happiness, as we shall see throughout the first half of this book.

Academic philosophy is first and foremost *a formal study of language.* Thus, if one were to claim 'the meaning of life' has plural meanings, his theory would be instantly disqualified as false or irrelevant because he failed to understand the inner workings of the English language; there is nothing in 'the meaning of life' denoting multiple meanings.[5] However, the well-known fact, concerning the difference between words in their plural and singular forms, did not stop philosophers from disregarding or misunderstanding the grammar of 'the meaning of life' anyway (e.g., Baggini, Cottingham, and Seachris). Another crucial omission has to do with Baggini ignoring the nuances of 'meaning' and Cottingham ignoring those of 'life,' and both issues are discussed in chapter 2 and addressed in chapter 6.

But of all the violations or omissions of grammar and semantics, the most serious and commonest one by far involves the definite article. The referential difference between *a* meaning of life and *the* meaning of life is nothing revelatory. If I asked a street merchant for "an apple," he would likely understand that I literally meant *any* apple would suffice; I am making an *indefinite* reference and not a definite one. However, if I pointed my finger and asked a street merchant for "the apple," he would still likely understand the specific apple I referenced. (Perhaps I wanted the only green apple on display.) Likewise, 'the meaning of life' does not refer to

5. Chapter 6 discusses the grammar rule barring multiple nuances of 'meaning' from applying to "meaning" in 'the meaning of life.' But that in itself does not necessarily preclude a pluralist from claiming that a single meaning has multiple sources while avoiding to claim that the meaning of life has multiple meanings.

just about any sort of meaning, but it does refer to one specifically. So, while that referential difference could understandably strike laypersons as "platitudinous," all but a handful of philosophers overlooked that single, grammatical detail, i.e., the definite article 'the.'[6] But the handful of philosophers who bothered describing the usage of 'the' clearly did not understand how grammar works, and neither did they reference any authoritative source from grammarians and lexicographers.[7]

In the formal-language-based discipline of philosophy, the omission of what seems so obvious comes at the highest theoretical cost: every theory mistaking the reference of "meaning" in 'the meaning of life' is technically disqualifiable. For if a theory is built around the wrong 'meaning,' it failed to answer the meaning of life completely.[8]

Still, neither the singular-plural distinction nor the definite-indefinite reference example is impressive on its own, as they are already tacitly known by most English speakers. But their leap from platitudinal to being more informative occurs with the answer to an ontological puzzle; without finding the ontologically necessary detail to the meaning of life—*whatever it is*—answering the life-problem correctly is impossible. I pause further discussion of the aforementioned ontological puzzle until my next mention of *Aristotle*.

Impossibilities play an integral part in how I construct defensive arguments relating to the answer to the meaning of life. For, as my experience has shown, there is never a shortage of adversaries willing to challenge my apodictic reasonings instead of admitting defeat. So, I shall demonstrate in chapters 4 and 5 the unpalatable *reductiones ad absurdum*, which result from the unjustified rejection of absolutes. For example, if a philosopher dismissed

6. The philosophers who noticed the definite article in the phrase 'the meaning of life' are Sharpe, Lurie, Seachris, and David Benatar.

7. I discuss this grammatical blunder in chapter 6.

8. I imagine that the same philosophers insisting on the there-are-no-right-answers cliché would ironically beseech a barista to pay better attention to their words, should the latter misunderstand their words and bring them the *wrong* beverage.

the literal interpretation of 'the meaning of life,' a *reductio ad absurdum* would introduce the scenario where any irrelevant claim could be uncritically asserted as its answer. Without a fixed and shared formal English meaning, 'the meaning of life' would cease to be an inquiry exclusively about itself and, instead, become one about anything, with the exception of self-contradictions. As a consequence, "What is the meaning of life?" would literally be indistinguishable from "is there a cat on the mat?" Let us now turn to how to disambiguate 'the meaning of life.'

To an inattentive mind, the distinction between the meaning of life and the purpose of life may escape forever unnoticed, since both 'meaning' and 'purpose' are sometimes—but not always—synonymous. Bob Sharpe, and J. J. C. Smart are few philosophers who explicitly distinguish between different nuances of 'meaning.' The former states that " 'meaning' is ambiguous. It can either be equivalent to 'significance' or it can connote 'purpose.' "[9] Similarly, Smart observed that "the English word 'meaning' has had two meanings: (1) 'purpose' or 'intention' and (2) that of word meaning. The second seems to have arisen from the first via the notion of the intention of the speaker."[10] However, the mentions of 'purpose,' by Sharpe, and 'purpose' and 'intention,' by Smart, are precisely the nuances that lead to conceptual confusions, which result in the aforementioned impossibilities I later exploit. As we shall see throughout this book, there are semantic and ontological differences between 'the meaning of life,' 'the purpose of life,' and the speaker's *intention* behind either's mention, which are distinct. What are some of these distinctions?

For any discussion of life's purpose to be possible, there must be some previous knowledge about the "life" in question. For example, we cannot discern whether a certain object is *for* playing volleyball without first knowing *what* the object in question is. From early on, most of us tacitly learned that volleyball requires a spherical ball of leather or synthetic leather, weighing nearly 300 grams with a circumference of roughly sixty-five centimeters;

9. Sharpe, "In Praise," para. 4.

10. Smart, "Meaning and Purpose," para. 1.

perhaps it is a Mikasa, but, in any case, the ball used for volleyball cannot be as hard as a basketball or as small as a tennis ball. Otherwise, the playability of volleyball would be diminished. Likewise, we cannot conceive of the question "what is the purpose of life?" without knowing the meaning of life. To understand the "ontological puzzle" I mentioned earlier, consider Aristotle's *Categories* wherein he states that "one is prior to two because if there are two it follows at once that there is one."[11] A question's meaning comes prior to its answer. If there is ever such a thing as life having a purpose, then it follows that life has meaning; without meaning, there is nothing for which we could determine its purpose in the same way there cannot be a game of volleyball without its leathery volleyball.

One does not have to be an Aristotelian philosopher to understand that a question, whose literal meaning is unknown, cannot be answered because its words would appear as a random assortment of unintelligible symbols. Otherwise, what would occur is the fallacy of affirming the consequent; after all, it is epistemically impossible for a philosopher to relevantly answer a question he does not understand. The two ontological puzzles presented in chapter 6 are therefore questions of what must *necessarily* occur prior to the act of solving the meaning of life.

While one may disagree that the meaning of life requires a careful reading, numerous and diverse errors committed by philosophers, as shown throughout this book, make it clear the life-problem thereof is greatly misunderstood. So, there is already sufficient justification for drawing attention to the grammar and semantics applicable to 'the meaning of life,' especially while philosophers fail to understand something as rudimentary as the definite article. In addition to the ontological priority, the linguistic method for discerning the meaning of 'the meaning of life' pinpoints to only one possible answer to the life-problem thereof. I shall argue in chapters 2–5 that the meaning of life is a problem of literal meaning, but I leave the powerful, ontological arguments for chapter 6.

11. 14a27–14b8.

I have, so far, provided some reasons for treating the meaning of life and the purpose of life as distinct problems, but what about Smart's reference 'meaning' implying 'intention'? What are the implications of determining 'the meaning of life' according to the intentions of the person raising the problem thereof?

The suggestion, idea, or claim that "what is the meaning of life?" is determined by its asker's intention leads to the following dilemma: is the answer to the meaning of life mind-dependent, or is it something independent of one's subjective makeup? If a philosopher equates the meaning of the meaning of life with how a person intends it, then he runs the risk of reducing a distinct problem into a psychological survey of ultimately indistinguishable perspectives and attitudes. At first glance, the claim that intention is relevant to the meaning of life may seem like an agreeable, people-friendly theory of life, and readers may welcome it. However, an intention-based theory of life cannot prevent irrelevant intentions from qualifying as the meaning of 'the meaning of life,' including ones that contradict the meaning of the life-problem thereof. To demonstrate its absurdity, I shall construct an intention-based theory of life in chapter 4, but I use the word 'perspective' in the place of 'intention'; in effect, intention-based theories are the same as the relativism I introduce therein.

Lastly, this "meaning," which appears quite prominently in the philosophy-of-life literature, requires more elaboration than merely stating its sources, such as God Almighty, "the originator of everything," or one's lifelong, philanthropic achievements. I shall therefore explain what other philosophers had expediently eschewed and dutifully take it upon myself to define what *exactly* the "meaning" in 'the meaning of life' means as I solve it.

I discussed the solution to the meaning of life sufficiently in this introductory chapter. We have now reached a point where it is time to direct our attention to a number of inconvenient and irrelevant philosopher-made problems, which are inimical to the inquiry's progress.[12]

12. The philosopher-made problems already discussed involve skepticism, grammatical oddities, ambiguity, intention-based meaning, and the lack of

IV

PHILOSOPHER-MADE PROBLEMS

As it currently stands, the philosophy of life is stagnated by ubiquitous unrelated areas of study, tangential speculations, and irrelevant obstacles. The unwieldy multifariousness of claims within this subdiscipline is such that it includes, but is not limited to, religion, naturalism, ethics, origin, aestheticism, existentialism, immortality, subjectivism, altruism, and worthwhile projects and achievements.

It is humanly impossible to assess the merits of each kind of claim pertaining to the meaning of life, as it would be a lifetime of commitment to summarize and analyze them all. For instance, in the searches I conducted in 2021 using my alma mater's online library database for the terms 'epistemology,' 'philosophy of mind,' 'ethics,' and 'the meaning of life,' the results showed 421,681, 1,774,372, 4,109,487, and 4,170,988 results, respectively.[13] For a field that has among the most mentions, the meaning of life is the most academically neglected area in philosophy, as I shall establish in forthcoming chapters.[14] Any hope to perusing philosophy-of-life literature for meaningful and relevant answers could be aptly

---

boundaries via ontological reasoning, which otherwise help distinguish one phrase from another.

13. The reader is encouraged to search key terms of philosophy in the "Search Omni Catalogue" box found on https://www.library.yorku.ca/web/. It should be noted that since York University Library's website's search function had improved a little after 2021 or so, the results have shrunk to a few hundred-thousand results per topic, but the philosophy of mind numbers over a million. However, the point about the meaning of life being a major area of interest in general, as opposed to being exclusively for philosophers, continues to hold true.

14. Despite my tactful pursuit and numerous correspondences with York University Library administration on several occasions, over the course of a few years, their intricate referral system, unhurried pace, reluctance to provide any feedback, and their selectiveness on keeping their promises to follow up with me has made obtaining permissions for the display of search results time-consuming and practically impossible.

summarized by E. O. Wilson's famous quote: "We are drowning in information, while starving for wisdom."[15]

One seemingly sensible approach is to circumnavigate copious and irrelevant literature for a clean slate in the philosophy of life. This was indeed Baggini's approach when he found that critically evaluating each theistic claim about the meaning of life in great detail was too time-consuming. If one chooses to focus on a new aspect of the philosophy-of-life discussion, it is possible to avoid retracing the steps in a beaten path that either lead in a circle or to a dead end.

However, misleading philosophy-of-life claims are unavoidable because they subtly introduce unnecessary obstacles to solving the meaning of life, so they must be addressed anyway; me avoiding or ignoring them will lend unmerited credence to philosopher-made problems as being "unsolvable" and rivaling theories as being "plausible" alternatives to my own. To solve the meaning of life, then, the philosophy of life must be cleared of its discursive literature; this shall require approaches for refuting all claims about the meaning of life.

Establishing many claims as being extraneous to the meaning of life requires exposing them for what they truly are: misleading, philosopher-made problems. There are several kinds of philosopher-made problems that I discuss in greater detail in chapters 2–4. One type of philosopher-made problems is perennial problems contemporary philosophers needlessly introduce to the philosophy of life. The commonest example of a perennial problem is the skepticism I mentioned from the very beginning; to avoid skepticism, I must avoid the use of empirical claims and any other kind of claim that lacks certainty and relevance to answering the meaning of life.

The second type of philosopher-made problems is truth-indeterminate propositions. For example, the atheists' claim that "God does not exist" is one that cannot be established as being true or false because of a lack of supporting evidence. Thus, the atheist's fundamental belief is indeterminate, even if, unbeknownst to us,

15. *Consilience*, 294.

mere humans, it is ultimately true or false. Without truth-determinacy, "God does not exist" will always face skepticism, which is an unnecessary perennial problem. Introducing claims favoring or disfavoring God's existence in the philosophy of life unnecessarily adds burdens of proof to a subdiscipline that already struggles with its own difficulties, such as semantic ambiguity.

The third type of philosopher-made problems is fallacies, which are often, but not always, the culprits behind the other two philosopher-made problems, i.e., perennial problems and truth-indeterminacies. Consider, once again, Smart's mention of the 'meaning' corresponding to "the intention of the speaker." If one were allowed to equate the intentions of a speaker with the meaning of life, then an appeal to subjectivity may result, a fallacy that occurs whenever a speaker contradicts things that we already implicitly know are true of the meaning of life. For example, I may intend "what is the meaning of life?" to mean "red," and for a theorist of intention-based meaning to remedy this patently false belief, he would have to introduce exclusionary criteria. However, by introducing non-negotiable guidelines for what constitutes relevant and irrelevant intentions for what the meaning of life should mean, the theorist of intention-based meaning has defeated his theory's purpose; the guidelines, if proven to be substantive, vitiate speakers' intentions as being necessary for 'the meaning of life' to be a meaningful phrase or question. But to avoid any question about whether the speaker-intention guidelines are unarbitrary or not, the theorist of intention-based meaning would have to eventually refer to the grammar and semantics of 'the meaning of life.' In any case, a speaker whose intention is rendered irrelevant by the aforesaid guideline could retort by reducing the theorist of intention-based meaning to a perspective and privilege all such claims as being incommensurable. I have now provided additional details of the *reductio ad absurdum* I advance in chapter 4.

The above example serves to demonstrate how an appeal to subjectivity begets perspectival relativism. With the perennial problem of relativism in play, all claims in the philosophy of life become mere "perspectives" and cannot be proved or disproved;

if appeals to subjectivity are left unchecked, any patently false or irrelevant belief about the meaning of life shall be exempted with the privileged status of a "perspective."

Although I know of no well-respected academician who seriously espouses the above caricatural example, perspectival relativism is nonetheless worthy of further consideration; the fecund grounds for brewing an irrepressible theory of relativism in the philosophy of life is a reliable testament of philosophers refusing to make use of pertinent facts or relevant analytic truths. I shall argue in chapters 3–4 that the absence of a relevant field of expertise results in a systematic stalemate of inquiries, resulting in a relativistic setting within the philosophy of life *de facto*. This is to say that, even as they would most certainly insist to be against relativism, philosophers' endless and irresolvable disagreements in the philosophy of life prove—as a matter of fact—otherwise. Should philosophers deny the seriousness of relativism, because it lacks overt proponents, I would certainly not mind adopting it if they should reject the relevant field of expertise I present in chapter 5. I shall likewise make use of other perennial problems, such as skepticism in chapter 4, for the sake of emphasizing the need for truth-certainty. The intent is to make the alternatives to my theory of life as unpalatable as possible, so that philosophers would lack the factual means for refuting relativism and the analytic, absolute truths for refuting skepticism.

Whereas I provided what *seems* to be a simplistic scenario of relativism, there are actually forms of reasoning in the philosophy of life so flawed they require no reduction on my part for being absurd on their own. Theism and secular theories of life are significantly responsible for philosopher-made problems because they represent a major portion of English publications in the philosophy of life in the Western Hemisphere. Let us briefly examine monotheism *per se* for the sake of illustrating other unnecessary difficulties philosophers introduce to the philosophy of life.

V

ABRAHAMIC MONOTHEISM

Every philosopher of life espousing Abrahamic monotheism is absolutely committed to the central thesis "God causes life to have meaning" and its implied fundamental proposition "God exists." But for the former statement to be true or false, the latter must be determined by either facts or analytic truths. However, it would be insufficient for God's existence to be proven by analytic truths alone, since theists are claiming *much* more than what mere words denote; God must *really* exist in the world. Consider René Descartes' comparison of God's essence to that of triangles and landscapes. He states that "existence can no more be separated from the essence of God than we can separate from the essence of a triangle that the sum of its three angles adds up to two right angles, or than we can separate the idea of a mountain from the idea of a valley."[16] Descartes continues more or less by claiming God cannot fail to exist because he is perfect, and existence is part of perfection. Conversely, as Descartes' argument goes, it is impossible for God to be absolutely perfect while nonexistent.

But, of all the philosophers who found kindred analytic reasonings of God's existence to those of Descartes's objectionable, it was Immanuel Kant, a theist, who adamantly denied that such a claim could ever be proved or disproved. He states: "Thus, while for the merely speculative employment of reason [*sic.*] the supreme being remains a mere *ideal*, [*sic.*] it is yet *an ideal without a flaw*, a concept which completes and crowns the whole of human knowledge. Its objective reality cannot indeed be proved, but also cannot be disproved, [*sic.*] by merely speculative reason."[17] In simpler words, the fundamental claim for all monotheistic theories of life cannot be determined through reason alone; if one were to attempt to establish that God exists in the *real world* through the sophistry of analytic reasoning, one would succeed only in

16. Descartes, *Meditations*, 47 (original: 66).
17. Kant, *A Critique*, A642/B670.

creating propositions with indeterminate truth-values. I shall further elaborate on these indeterminacies in chapter 3.

If Kant is correct in denying that God's existence could be established, over and above one's faith in his existence, then it does not matter how sophisticated a monotheistic philosopher's argument is. Even if one delivered the best argument favoring a monotheistic claim about the meaning of life, its effect is essentially null without an actual God rather than merely an analytically true definition of 'God.' Analytic arguments favoring God's existence would thus fail to translate into evaluable empirical statements or (relevant) analytic statements about the meaning of life. But these epistemic woes are not only limited to supernatural claims about the meaning of life, they also apply equally to aesthetic, ethics, subjectivist, objectivist, altruist theories of life, and many more.

VI

SUMMARY

Insofar as many types of claims bring with them taxing burdens of proof, it is thus possible to refute all theories of life (by type) that fail to meet them. If a theory meets its burden of proof or lacks the need to meet one, there are other grounds in which they are refuted; I mentioned earlier technical grounds on which a theory contradicts what 'the meaning of life' denotes, fails to address it relevantly and meaningfully, or raises unassailable and unnecessary philosopher-made problems. So, relevance is another theme I explore throughout the forthcoming chapters.

For the first five chapters of this book, I shall focus mainly on the technical flaws of contemporary theories of life, which compete against the one I advance in chapter 6. As the book progresses, the intensity of the consequences stemming from philosopher-made problems shall worsen to a point where the only way for progress to occur is by rejecting all contemporary theories of life; by chapter 5's conclusion, it shall be clear that solving the meaning of life requires a new start with all the recommendations I make, based on avoiding kindred mistakes committed by philosophers of life presented throughout this book.

I shall solve the meaning of life when I am completely assured that all obstacles that are irrelevant to solving the meaning of life are avoided or defeated.

Chapter 2

How to Spot Nonsense

IN THIS CHAPTER, I shall answer the three following questions. First, how is it possible that so many knowledgeable and otherwise capable academicians failed to address 'the meaning of life' relevantly and meaningfully? Second, how could we be sure that all claims about the meaning of life are faulty if little to nothing is known about it? Third, what are the characteristics of the answer that completely solves the meaning of life? If I am right in posing these questions and the implicit suspicions are correct, then the need for a respectable, unarbitrary, intersubjective, and scientific means of agreement in the philosophy of life should be increasingly evident.[1]

Philosopher-made problems are fallacies, indeterminacies, or perennial problems leading to or resulting from the claims that writers, thinkers, theorists, or philosophers, in particular, advance. In every case, philosopher-made problems are rooted in the assumptions academicians hastily make about the ill-defined problem of 'the meaning of life.' Although discerning which claims are faulty from correct ones is a monumentally challenging task, given that the life-problem is not sufficiently well-understood, indeterminacies and perennial problems are the most noticeable

---

1. By "need," I mean the introduction of a relevant field of expertise with commonly accepted facts to settle disagreements within the philosophy of life; I shall elaborate on the field thereof in chapter 5 and 6, since I leave indeterminacies, religion, and subjectivism for discussion in chapters 3, and 4.

outcomes of fallacious reasoning. However, fallacies are harder to notice than other types of philosopher-made problems. Like the Trojan horse's role in the fall of Troy, fallacies are rooted in deeply entrenched assumptions we uncritically accept about what the meaning of life seems to entail. But we must guard ourselves against our biases if we should finally learn the truth about the meaning of life. One recurring example of a fallacy, that of equivocation, is a tendency among even the more noteworthy and experienced academicians to interchange blindly between 'meaning,' 'purpose,' and 'worthwhile.'

It would be impossible within an ordinary lifespan to evaluate ubiquitous claims made by every theorist to point out what misled their reasoning. However, the tedium of addressing each publication concerning the meaning of life is unnecessary. For there is a general pattern of illogical reasonings that can be extrapolated from even a very limited sample of claims. Philosophers are unable to learn from the mistakes of others and, thus, repeat them; the only creative variation of these mistakes is their expression in different words. That extrapolation shall serve in drawing an implicit "taxonomy" of problems that are "endemic" to the meaning of life. In short, I shall take up claims advanced by some of the most eminent thinkers and examine where their inquiries faltered, and then later use the "taxonomy" to gingerly avert kindred illogical reasonings.

I

HOW TO KNOW THE QUESTION BEING ANSWERED

Consider the similarity between baking a pastry and answering "what is the meaning of life?" As almost any baker of any skill knows or should know, the very first step to making pastry requires knowing which pastry to make. For instance, if the meaning of life is a *particular* chocolate cake, then we need to know we are preparing *this* chocolate cake, as opposed to another pastry, before gathering ingredients and any necessary appliances. Otherwise, we would be at a loss for which ingredients and appliances are applicable. Likewise, we need to know what exactly the question "what is the meaning of life?" demands before proceeding to answer it; otherwise, we risk answering a wholly different question than the one originally intended. (The reader may recall one's *understanding of a question* as being ontologically prior to his *ability to answer it* in the first chapter.)

However, the obviousness of needing to know what pastry is being made or, rather, what the meaning of life demands has eluded every philosopher to date. Many significant publications in the philosophy of life have not articulated what each one's author means by "life," "meaning," or "purpose," or other related terms vis-à-vis the big questions; for example, are philosophers correct in presuming that 'meaning' and 'purpose' are synonymous? An attentive reading of Richard Taylor, John Kekes, William Lane Craig, John Cottingham, and Julian Baggini reveals a complete disregard for defining the main life-question. But it would be a considerable waste of space to name hundreds of other, lesser-known authors who likewise omit the original life-question, since their influences are too negligible to affect the philosophy of life. Some fairly influential authors that I named have ignored the standard and well-known academic practice—as old as philosophy itself—of defining a given inquiry's main problem or question and its key words. If left unscrutinized, the writings of someone as influential as a president of the Aristotelian Society could mislead a subdiscipline in philosophy for generations.

Let us turn to Cottingham, and Baggini for a few superb examples of omission and equivocation. The former dubbed his book *On the Meaning of Life* after the namesake problem he tried answering. If it were a pastry, then we at least know by *name* the problem Cottingham had in mind for solving; this is a comparatively decent start for an inquiry, since, by contrast, Baggini was unclear about which of several life-problems he was addressing at various points throughout his book.[2]

2. As its title indicates, Baggini's book *What's it All About?: Philosophy*

In his introduction, Baggini claimed the question "[w]hat's it all about?" "is not so much a single question but a place-holder for a whole set of questions: Why are we here? What is the purpose of life? Is it enough just to be happy?"[3] etc. This elucidation was excellent in the beginning because Baggini made clear what he meant by his use of "[w]hat's it all about?" However, he only goes as far as to distinguish the ambiguity of "[w]hy are we here?" as being either "the *causes* of why we are here" or "the *purpose* of our existence."[4] We are, alas, left with guessing Baggini's use of other words, such as "meaning" and "purpose" vis-à-vis 'the meaning of life' and 'the purpose of life.' Worse, Baggini never explicitly stated whether he believes the aforementioned problems of meaning and purpose are the same or different. He does, for instance, interchange between "the meaning of life" and "what gives life purpose and value" by "reducing the vague, mysterious question"[5] of the former to a series of questions of the latter. Does he believe "what is the meaning of life?" is also a "place-holder" within the original placeholder question "[w]hat is it all about"? It certainly seems so, as the reducibility of a whole to its parts is equivalent to the-meaning-of-life placeholder and the sub-questions the what-is-it-all-about "place-holder" comprises.

Even if a question is reducible to a bundle of other questions, that does not absolve Baggini of the duty to tell his readers which life-question he is addressing at any particular point. Instead, Baggini leaves a rather large word salad for his readers to decipher. For instance, five of his six sources of the meaning of life imply objects of pursuit, i.e., objects that a person must actively pursue to attain. Whereas only one of these sources seems closer to how we may

---

and the Meaning of Life is too vague; he makes no effort to explain to readers whether the meaning of life is central to his general question (i.e., "What's it all about?"), or whether it is a peripheral topic. The issue of ambiguity shall be central to my criticisms of Baggini's theory of life.

3. *What's It All About*, 1.

4. *What's It All About*, 6.

5. Baggini, *What's It All About*, 185.

describe something as having *significance* or something distinct from the act of pursuing an object.

The "values" (or, more appropriately, pursuits) of happiness, success, seizing the day, helping others live meaningfully, and love, which Baggini named, [6] were not sufficiently unpacked for the sake of perspicuity. 'Value' is a term that literally implies 'worthwhile,' and the five aforementioned sources, as self-evidently requiring action on the part of a person to attain them, are equivalent to the usual philosophy-of-life idiom 'worthwhile pursuits.' Or, more poignantly, they may be called *worthwhile purposes*. The remaining source is an appreciation of pleasures in life, and that, in itself, emphasizes aesthetics and, thus, the *significance* of an object; in other words, that last source Baggini named is semantically closer to a different nuance of 'meaning,' which has to do with 'what something is,' as opposed to 'what something is for.'[7] Aesthetics is defined as "a set of principles concerned with the nature and appreciation of beauty, especially in art,"[8] which, as one of Baggini's sources of meaning, differs from worthwhile pursuits; these "principles" thereof, which are implicit in the Kierkegaardian idea of 'aesthetics' that Baggini explicitly borrows, have more to do with concepts rather than with worthwhile pursuits or purposes. These two distinct meanings of 'meaning,' between what something is and what something is for, require Baggini to clarify how 'the meaning of life,' a phrase making a singular reference, possibly allows for two different homonyms simultaneously. The appreciation of pleasure most closely corresponds to the first homonym of 'meaning' below, whereas the five values Baggini lists are of the second unmistakeably:

1. "what is meant by a word, text, concept, or action,"[9] and

---

6. *What's It All About*, 188.

7. Baggini's use of "aesthetics" is borrowed from Søren Kierkegaard's *Fear and Trembling* (1941 [1843]) and should not be mistaken for its more usual associations with respect to art, poetry, beauty, and the like.

8. *Concise Oxford Dictionary*, 10th ed. (1999), s.v. "aesthetics."

9. *Concise Oxford Dictionary*, 10th ed. (1999), s.v. "meaning."

2. "worthwhile quality; purpose."[10]

Since 'the meaning of life' that Baggini *explicitly* addresses is singular and does not denote more than one meaning, his theory is mistaken for implying its answer is simultaneously (1) and (2).[11]

Wherever Baggini failed to consistently name the problems he discussed, Cottingham succeeded. But, to put my analogy to further use, what of the "pastry" itself? Our "baker," Cottingham, leaves us in the dark about whether the particular "chocolate cake" presented is, in fact, the same "pastry" he named. He loosely defines the meaning of life below:

> If the argument at the end of the last chapter is sound, to be truly meaningful that journey must reflect not just any old purposes or projects we happen to adopt, but those that are genuinely worthwhile. We cannot bestow meaning on our lives just by floundering after individual gratification, nor can we create value merely by our own insistent choices, made without regard for the conditions of our (interdependent) flourishing as human beings. A worthwhile life will be one that possesses genuine value

10. *Concise Oxford Dictionary*, 10th ed. (1999), s.v. "meaning."

11. But Baggini may avoid the technical fault of proposing multiple meanings for a problem that unmistakably demands a single meaning; he may deny the apparent equivocation of differing homonyms of 'meaning' by clarifying his use of aesthetics as being the same type of meaning as the other aforementioned five sources of meaning. That is, if it is assumed rather charitably that the five other sources of meaning he named, excluding aesthetics, are of the *same* type; it remains an open question, after all, whether Baggini's multiple sources of meaning contradict a question (i.e., "What is the meaning of life?") that explicitly demands an answer for the single meaning it references. If Baggini were to claim that the aforementioned sources of meanings are of different types, then the charge of equivocation would hold, and his theory would be technically false. However, if he were to insist on multiple meanings of a single kind of meaning, then he would be in a defensible position; he would be able to argue that he had not contradicted the singular "meaning" in 'the meaning of life' by advancing a theory of multiple sources meanings that are all of a single kind of meaning. But aside from equivocations, I shall bring attention to another issue with Baggini's theory of life in the following chapter, which is quite problematic. For now, Baggini's equivocation of "meaning" in 'the meaning of life' rests on how exactly he defines his six sources of meaning or, likely, *meanings*.

> – value linked to our human nature and the pursuit of
> what is objectively conducive to the flowering of that
> nature.[12]

One should find curious Cottingham's closely assimilated words "truly meaningful," "worthwhile life," and "the pursuit of what is objectively conducive to the flowering of" "our human nature." Is Cottingham equating 'the meaning of life' with "a worthwhile life"? Based on the above paragraph, Cottingham made the implicit claim that a meaningful life, *qua* the meaning of life, must be a "worthwhile life."[13] Furthermore, a worthwhile life is one that possesses "value linked to our human nature" and pursuits that *genuinely* improve our human nature.[14] It syllogistically follows, then, that the meaning of life is partially dependent on certain pursuits that objectively improve, by "flowering," our human nature; the other partial dependency being the "value linked to our human nature." But the erstwhile Aristotelian Society president had not explained how life is "truly meaningful," *qua* 'the meaning of life,' through these "pursuits" and "not just any old purposes or projects." It is equally possible, on the basis of "what is the meaning of life?" being an open question, that the meaning of life is not necessarily a worthwhile life; it may not even involve any pursuits whatsoever, as we see with definition (1) of 'meaning.'

12. Cottingham, *On the Meaning*, 32.

13. I had to emphasize "a meaningful life" as being "the meaning of life" because the two phrases are not always the same semantically. However, in this particular case, Cottingham intended for the former to mean the latter, so my clarification was appropriate given the ambiguity.

14. The awkward language of having to constantly specify "meaningful" or other variants of the word 'meaning' as pertaining to 'the meaning of life' is necessary for avoiding any semantic changes, which may cause confusion. For instance, the phrase 'life's meaning' is similar to 'the meaning of life,' but the two phrases do not necessarily have the same meaning-reference. This is due to the latter phrase having a definite article; I elaborate on the relationship between a phrase or a question's wording and its answer in chapter 6. If "meaningful" has any other meaning than the meaning of "meaning" in 'the meaning of life,' then we would be confronted by a different problem, which would be beyond the scope of this book.

Cottingham did not explain within his book why the meaning of life is worthwhile and why it includes pursuits that ultimately improve our human nature. Neither did Cottingham elaborate on whether his mention of certain "worthwhile" *pursuits* (or purposes, rather) means he is treating 'the meaning of life' and 'the purpose of life' as the same philosophical problem. Nor has he elaborated on which homonym of 'life' he is referencing. We know that there are at least several homonyms at play:

A. "the condition that distinguishes animals and plants from inorganic matter, including the capacity for growth, functional activity, and continual change preceding death";[15]

B. "the existence of an individual human being or animal,"[16] and

C. "spirit, animation."[17]

First, Cottingham's example of "Alan, a golfer," as living "a meaningful life, or some meaning, to his life" because he is "happily absorbed in their [his] own favoured pursuits [pursuit]"[18] implies neither (A) nor (B) of 'life.' Cottingham is not describing the anatomical (A) or ontological (B) aspect of Alan's life. In fact, there is absolutely no mention of Alan's salvation for his existence or his health, which would imply (B) or (A), respectively. Cottingham is instead referring to a "structure" and "easy flow to life," which have to do with routine and having affluence. This is to say, "Alan is comfortably off" and "feels satisfied"[19] when he does well in golf. These descriptions strongly suggest the nuance of 'life' implied by Cottingham's example of Alan as living a supposedly meaningful life is *prudential* rather than physiological (A) or ontological (B). Therefore, the *most applicable* definition for Cottingham's aforementioned use of "life," if at all, is (C).

---

15. *Concise Oxford Dictionary*, 10th ed. (1999), s.v. "life."

16. *Concise Oxford Dictionary*, 10th ed. (1999), s.v. "life."

17. *Merriam-Webster*, s.v. "life (*n.*)," definition 10, https://www.merriam-webster.com/dictionary/life.

18. *On the Meaning*, 19.

19. *On the Meaning*, 19.

Second, we know the word 'death,' as in Cottingham's use of the phrase "inevitability of death,"[20] is the termination of (A) and, if there is no afterlife, (B) as well. Cottingham does use the word "mortality," following the "inevitability of death," so we know (A) is, by definition, necessarily implied. In other words, a living person may die in terms of (A), but a person's attitudes toward life cannot; rather, if a person dies, their thoughts and feelings about anything come to an end, and this is the strict semantic difference that separates (C) from (A) and (B). The differences highlighted in this paragraph and the previous one mean Cottingham used more than one homonym of 'life' and has committed multiple equivocations between them.

Each time Cottingham swaps a homonym of 'life,' he is inquiring about a new, separate, and distinct the-meaning-of-life problem. Under *some* linguistic circumstances, the interchange of homonyms is usually unproblematic. However, multiple phrases with identical words, morphology, and syntax are not always the same semantically; their differing contexts may alter the applicability of certain homonyms, especially with commonly nuanced words, such as 'meaning' and 'life.' Did Cottingham intend to address one or multiple different nuances of 'life' whenever he referenced 'the meaning of life'? Here, Cottingham stumbled into the same issue as Baggini because the "meaning" in 'the meaning of life' is singular, and thus it limits the numbers of applicable homonyms of "life" to a single one. The two terms, i.e., "meaning" and "life" in 'the meaning of life,' covary, after all. But even if we granted Cottingham's use of 'life' was intended as a mass noun, implying many or all lives, that term would nevertheless be *one* kind of meaning.

If the intentions of both authors were to address multiple meanings of life, then they must rephrase the question to suit whatever it is they are trying to address, e.g., 'the *meanings* of life.' The singular-plural distinction just mentioned is a detail that even

---

20. *On the Meaning*, 36.

David Benatar noticed.[21][22] But suppose for the sake of argument, Cottingham and all the said authors elaborated on their particular uses of key words, such as "life," "meaning," and "purpose" and their related cognates and perceived synonyms; suppose, moreover, philosophers of life explained why they interchange these terms: we would still be nowhere nearer to finding out what the meaning of life truly is.

Even if the authors explained their use of key terms, such an attempt would be futile since their chosen definitions do not correspond with the actual meaning of the life-problems' words anyway. Perhaps, for example, the possibility of nuance Cottingham ignored turns out true, and 'the meaning of life' has nothing to do with the presumption that it must entail a worthwhile life. If "meaning" in 'the meaning of life' implies definition (1), then any claim implying (2) is false. For instance, "meaning" in 'the meaning of life' would denote, "[W]hat is meant by a word, text..." but not "worthwhile quality; purpose." If so, Cottingham's description of a worthwhile life, however eloquent it may appear, would fail from the outset in addressing the original question, "What is the meaning of life?" Cottingham's book would instead be one that describes what he *thinks* is *a* worthwhile life but not *the* meaning of life, whether he intends it or not. The former (i.e., what Cottingham thinks) is up to interpretation because it is indefinite, unspecific, and open-ended, but the latter (i.e., what is, in fact, *the* meaning of life) is not, since it is preceded by a *definite article*. In any case, the theories of Baggini, and Cottingham are technically false for their plural uses of 'meaning' and 'life' when addressing the life-problem that denotes a single meaning.

21. See *The Human Predicament*, 63.

22. See section I of chapter 3 for a quote belonging to Benatar on the singular-plural distinction.

II

THE WORST POSSIBLE MISTAKE

The most error-prone point in solving the meaning of life is the stage at which it is being defined; most philosophers, especially those of the analytic tradition, ignore the slight nuances of key words, as we saw with Baggini, and Cottingham. If a question is misunderstood as a result of ill-definition, then its answer would almost certainly fail to address the question relevantly and mean-ingfully, no matter how well-reasoned the theory superficially appears. It would be similar to knowing *a question is being asked* without knowing *what is being asked,* and such an unwitting an-swer, in this case, would be no more than a blind guess; it would be no different than basing one's retirement plan on a random-pick lottery ticket. Blind guesses in philosophy almost never work. But in the most unlikely scenario where a guess turns out true, the philosopher cannot repeat (by generalizing) the reasoning or justify its truth, much less know it for certain. The answer to the first question posed at the beginning of this chapter is: every philosopher to this day completely misunderstood the answer to 'the meaning of life' because of their unwillingness to study its lan-guage. Let us now turn to the reason philosophers are so unwilling to study the language of 'the meaning of life.'

As a deceased philosophy professor explained, "no where [*sic.*] in my philosophical studies had I confronted the question of the meaning of life."[23] Neither had Adams seriously confronted the life-problem during his fifty years as a professor, even as he taught "Moral Philosophy and The Meaning of Life." I mentioned in the previous chapter that 'the meaning of life' is as active a literary topic as other major subdisciplines in philosophy, such the episte-mology. However, the meaning of life receives fewer participants among analytic philosophers. And even then, those among the philosophers who occasionally write on the philosophy of life are too eager to hurry its answer without giving it an afterthought.

23. Adams, "The Meaning of Life," 71.

The deafening silence on the original life-question and lack of due seriousness toward it was and, unfortunately, still is the prevailing attitude among analytic philosophers, including Adams' by his own admission. He recalled when he "heard a distinguished analytic philosopher confess rather apologetically, in his presidential address to the American Philosophical Association, that once in a time of weakness and lapse of judgement [*sic.*] he wrote a paper on the meaning of life."[24]

The sardonic mockery of an inquiry by the unnamed, influential figure would not have taken place if the person thereof truly understood it. It is as Richard Taylor writes:

> The question whether life has any meaning is difficult to interpret, and the more one concentrates his critical faculty on it the more it seems to elude him, [*sic.*] or to evaporate as any [*sic.*] intelligible question. One wants to turn it aside, as a source of embarrassment, as something that, if it cannot be abolished, should at least be decently covered.[25]

But this was as far as Taylor's opening commentary rang true; he was mistaken in concluding that the question concerning the meaning of life lacks an objective answer or, at the very least, the possibility of being knowable in a non-subjective way. As he phrased it, the "meaning of life is from within us, it is not bestowed from without."[26] However, I remain unconvinced that Taylor has made an appropriate excuse for dismissing a more objective answer to the meaning of life outright; he had merely advanced an *unargued assertion.* Neither is one's embarrassment, from what he *perceives* as perplexing, nor what he perceives as unintelligible *sufficient* for the life-problem's dismissal, as we saw with the president Adams refused to name. And whether or not one is truly embarrassed or impatiently declaring a verdict on the inquiry's solvability, the privilege of casting aside a problem as "meaningless" is one that must be earned. For it is uncharacteristic and unbecoming

24. Adams, "The Meaning of Life," 71.
25. "The Meaning of Life," 167.
26. Taylor, "The Meaning of Life," 175.

of philosophers to discard or underestimate a question of grand importance without at least giving it a proper literal reading. Philosophy is, first and foremost, a study of words and meanings; without a modicum of linguistics, there can never be a philosophy of anything. Only then, when its words fail to denote significance, will analytic philosophers have earned the privilege to dismiss the life-problem in question.

Bearing Taylor's assumptions in mind: does 'the meaning of life' fail to mean anything non-subjectively or "from without"? And should this problem be established as non-subjectively meaningful, why do philosophers *still* insist on refusing, or implicitly refuse, to examine it literally?[27]

Unlike Taylor, and Baggini, Cottingham mentioned the study of language as a possible means for inquiring about the meaning of life and was also very quick to do so. However, Cottingham nonetheless insisted that the meaning of "words or sentences or propositions" would lead one into treating the meaning of life as "a sign of conceptual confusion."[28] Adams likewise believed that meaning only pertains "to the semantics of language and symbol systems," which "led [him] to think that there was a category mistake in talking about the meaning of life."[29] But neither philosopher explained why such a literal reading of the problem would entail dismissing it as being nonsensical or a category-mistake.[30] Nowhere in 'the meaning of life' is there the sort of patent nonsense or contradiction that is found in "this sentence is false" or Noam Chomsky's "[c]olorless green ideas sleep furiously."[31] So, both philosophers need to provide more than a mere assertion for why linguistics is inappropriate for solving the meaning of life.

27. After all, if a problem has a literal meaning, then that meaning thereof is conventional and non-subjective.

28. *On the Meaning*, 2.

29. Adams, "The Meaning of Life," 71.

30. "Category-mistake" is exactly how Gilbert Ryle, the philosopher who introduced the term in *The Concept of Mind* (1949), spells it, which is why I continue in using the term with the hyphen.

31. *Syntactic Structures*, 15.

Although Cottingham never explicitly dismissed language-based reasoning, he mentioned the incommensurability between "words or sentences or propositions" and "objects or events in the world, like the lives of trees, or lobsters, or humans."[32] But what if 'the meaning of life' is strictly a study of language *and nothing else*? The possible exclusion of objects or events in the world, however unpalatable to our uncritically held biases about the meaning of life, is not a strike against language as providing its true answer. Once again, Cottingham is rushing an assumption about a question whose answer has yet to be known; it is plainly wrong to make an assertion from a position of ignorance. So, for all that is currently known, the answer to the meaning of life may or may not entail worldly objects or events. But we could make that determination once the meaning of life is properly framed.

As for the rest of Cottingham's book, the possibility of framing 'the meaning of life' according to conventional English usage was quietly shrugged away. He instead emphasized "religious discourse" for "addressing what cannot fully be put into words, at least the words of our rational scientific culture, but which can still somehow be shown, disclosed, made manifest."[33]

To answer the first of two questions in section II, neither philosopher has shown that the meaning of life cannot possess non-subjective meaning through the words it comprises. In fact, formal academic inquiries on this subject would be impossible if not for the denotative meanings of words the problem carries; I cannot otherwise imagine an inquiry being socially possible or intelligibly communicable without the agreed-upon usage of significant symbols, which is necessary to a shared, conventional, natural language such as English. This means that, for the second question, Cottingham, and Adams did not provide sufficient reason for dismissing a literal interpretation of 'the meaning of life'; they did not understand how rudimentary linguistics forms an integral part of philosophizing analytically. As we shall see in chapter 5, the handful of philosophers who were also, in some rather limited

32. *On the Meaning*, 2.

33. Cottingham, *On the Meaning*, 9.

capacity, aware of linguistics had likewise cast aside its obvious and indispensable usefulness without fair argument.

The "rational scientific culture" Cottingham rejected as being explanatorily insufficient for "what cannot fully be put into words" is merely one kind of science, i.e., the physical sciences; the inapplicability of one kind of science does not necessitate the exclusion of another. For instance, linguistics is not always a physical science, except branches like phonetics with respect to the positions of the lips, tongue, teeth, and the overall use of the vocal apparatus. Linguistics is, instead, a family of sciences involving the study of abstractions, which are nonphysical and irreducible to physics. These abstractions include concepts or ideas embedded within the symbols we know as alphabets, morphemes, words, phrases, sentences, etc., and their contemporary and historical usages. Thus, Cottingham is mistaken in either treating all the sciences as being categorically the same or failing to clarify how they are *all* insufficient for inquiring about the meaning of life. We could clearly see 'the meaning of life' itself as being a collection of words with meaning; literal meaning *literally* qualifies as 'meaning.' But without language, we have nothing intelligible to inquire. Also, the claim that the meaning of life is partly ineffable is moot, and Cottingham has in no way established his claim credibly; the practice of rituals, meditations, and prayers he had in mind for "religious discourse" does not prove the meaning of life cannot be fully put into words, much less be its source of meaning. In well-practiced philosophy, which is concomitant with logically valid arguments, the reasoning begins at the premises and not the conclusion; Cottingham's hasty rejection of linguistics is therefore question-begging.

So far, there is not a single reason provided for disregarding the meaning of life as being literally definable and explicable through formal English linguistics. The philosopher who, I believe, came closest to arguing against some measure of linguistics is none other than R. W. Hepburn (1966). But similar to Cottingham's hurried dismissal of "scientific culture," Hepburn had only succeeded in drawing a strawman fallacy in the most spectacular of ways. We shall revisit those I dub "anti-linguists" in chapter 5 and explore further the recalcitrance of philosophers for appropriately defining the meaning of life.

In the three forthcoming chapters, we shall see why exactly the omission of defining a problem properly is the worst possible mistake when inquiring about the meaning of life.

III

THE ANSWERS TO THE THREE MAIN QUESTIONS

I have thus far shown two standards of inquiring about the meaning of life that ought to have been obvious among analytic philosophers. First, the theorist addressing multiple, distinct life-problems must explicitly state which among them is currently being discussed each time his inquiry takes on a new theme or topic; this way, the reader is not forced to guess the author's intentions. In short, theorists must explicitly *name the problem*. Second, the theorist must *lexically* define the applicable nuances of key words within a life-problem, explain his choices, and refrain from indiscriminately interchanging between semantically different homonyms; this is especially true of the "meaning" in 'the meaning of life' being singular, since its morphology precludes the use of multiple meanings for itself, and the same is true of its covariant "life." In short, theorists must explicitly *define the problem*.

Returning to the second question posed from the very beginning of this chapter, the answer to the life-problem is not known as of yet, but an answer that contradicts its grammar and semantics is indubitably false; the absoluteness in this case, as I shall explain in the forthcoming chapters—especially chapter 6—has to do with analytic truths pertaining to 'the meaning of life.' For instance, Baggini, and Cottingham cannot apply two homonyms of 'meaning' or 'life' to a singular word reference denoted by 'the meaning of life'; that is otherwise the equivalent of stating, for example, "One (meaning) is equal to two (meanings)," which is patently false because it is literally and logically impossible.

As for the third question, the true answer to the meaning of life has the characteristics of concomitantly adhering to the conventional rules of English and the aforementioned standards of inquiry, i.e., naming and defining the inquiry or problem; the conventional rules of English are discussed in chapter 5, but the standards of inquiry are applied to my reasonings from this point onward. Whatever is lexically denoted by 'the meaning of life' functions as the boundaries that set apart an answer qualifying as relevant to it from those that are irrelevant.

But the faults in the above theories may be remedied by theorists willing to drop all references of inapplicable homonyms. For example, Cottingham could opt for inquiring 'the meaning of life' *qua* significance instead of pursuits (purpose) or the converse, as long as he does not choose both. He must likewise choose which 'life' he intends for "life" in 'the meaning of life,' such as one that involves either attitude (C), biology (A), existence (B), etc. Baggini likewise has a choice between retaining the five worthwhile pursuits he calls "values" ('meaning,' definition 2) or the stand-alone source of significance ('meaning,' definition 1). But he cannot choose both kinds of meanings simultaneously for a question (i.e., "What is the meaning of life?") that explicitly requires a *single* meaning for its answer.

IV

CONCLUSION

From the beginning of this chapter, I mentioned that the need for a respectable, unarbitrary, intersubjective, and scientific means of agreement in the philosophy of life *should* be increasingly evident, especially by now. It is no secret, after all, that philosophers of life are currently unable to agree on how 'the meaning of life' should be interpreted and answered; for instance, Cottingham believes the meaning of life involves spiritual or religious exercise and a belief in God; Baggini believes plural sources of *meanings* varying from *carpe diem* (i.e., "seizing the day") to aesthetics (i.e., contemplating or appreciating certain experiences), and Taylor believes the meaning of life is "from within," as in being subjectively dependent on a person's attitude toward his life. Clearly, then, there are too many unrelated themes of inquiry discussed vis-à-vis the meaning of life, and this raises the worry that the life-problem is becoming too enigmatic and ill-defined to be properly answered. "The worst possible mistake" references what I mentioned in chapter 1, wherein "what is the meaning of life?" loses its literal value and becomes indiscernible from "is the cat on the mat?" This shall be proved through the reductiones ad absurdum in chapters 4–5.

Without an agreed-upon foundation, the unassailable disagreements will continue to obfuscate how one could meaningfully, relevantly, truly, and perspicuously interpret the meaning of life and answer it. However, I do not expect the reasons I thus far presented sufficiently compelling; for even as the theories of life examined in this chapter are technically false because they literally fail to address the meaning of life, my adversaries are likely unconvinced.

I anticipate philosophers would be inclined to dismiss the usefulness of rudimentary linguistics as nothing more than a profligate exercise of pedantry instead of giving it any sincere consideration. For instance, we saw that Adams, and Cottingham did little more than briefly mention the subject of language in their first few pages before moving on with what they believed worthy of consideration; they did not even think it necessary to explicitly reject the study of language because they underestimated it as a serious alternative to their own views. There shall be additional instances of other philosophers, those I dub "anti-linguists," adopting a very dismissive attitude toward the study of language in chapter 5. But for what is plainly the case as of now, philosophers discoursing the meaning of life do not believe this is the sort of problem that must be understood literally. So, I, therefore, have more reason to further demonstrate contemporary theories of life as being misguided and false or, if not immediately refutable, indeterminate and nonsensical; only, this time, I shall do so with my hands tied behind my back by foregoing the use of linguistics for the most part of chapter 3. I shall further demonstrate in the three forthcoming chapters that remedying faulty theories—such as the ones I proposed for Baggini, and Cottingham—is futile since they are fundamentally flawed and usually truth-indeterminate.

Once all rivaling theories of life are completely vitiated, I shall reveal the authoritative field of expertise for solving the meaning of life in chapter 5 and then methodically apply it in chapter 6.

Chapter 3

Deus ex Machina

Let us suppose, as is most likely the case, my adversaries wish to circumnavigate the bare use of linguistics. We need to know then: What are the viable alternatives to linguistics for solving the meaning of life? Based on how indispensable some rudimentary linguistics is for framing problems well, it is incumbent upon anti-linguists to provide a better-suited alternative to one that already shows promising potential for solving the meaning of life. Even seventh-graders are taught that the first rule of science involves *defining a problem.* For it would be self-defeating to reject the age-old linguistic method of naming and defining a problem by its strict literal meaning, only to have nothing useful to contribute in its stead. Theism is one alternative, and the other is subjectivism: both views are infamously recalcitrant toward standards of inquiry, which must apply to all theories evenly. The former view shall increasingly be my focus herein, whereas the latter shall serve as a reductio ad absurdum in chapter 4. But it shall be increasingly evident by the end of this chapter that there are no shortcuts to defining the life-problem; language is *inextricably* fundamental to the meaning of life.

Even as theorists posit life's meaning as being either magnificently above and beyond mere words or trivially relative, no claim can be articulated intelligibly without being properly expressed in the language it appears. Neither is it an intellectually satisfying excuse for philosophers to otherwise insist the meaning of life need not be intelligible or explainable. This lazy "rebuttal" to my recommendation of the linguistic method is not an answer at all. Lest the discipline should live up to its lamentable reputation as being little more than speculation, mellifluous ideals, and the disconsolate profligacy of ink, effort, and time, the act of philosophizing must lead somewhere. Whether life is meaningful in virtue of divine fiat or by individual choice and preference, the meaning of life is entirely dependent on its literal content. However, I cannot help but doubt philosophers of life would readily accept an incontrovertibly well-argued view, should it obliterate their deeply entrenched beliefs. For it is in the nature of philosophers to be pugnacious, even as such a gratuitous propensity lacks any gainful purpose.

Should philosophers injudiciously defy the language underlying the meaning of life, they must sincerely reconsider the theory-crippling consequences of their willful ignorance. As we had previously seen with Baggini's, and Cottingham's gross equivocations of nuanced words, the misinterpretation of ill-defined problems begets more fallacies, such as question-begging and non-sequitur, and other philosopher-made problems, such as truth-indeterminacies. Unless the goal of philosophizing is to reason faultily, the oversight of what 'the meaning of life' denotes must come to an end.

We shall see by chapter 4's conclusion that the way forward requires jettisoning all contemporary theories of life, especially while some have had centuries for proving their worth. Yet all of them still amounted to nothing but nonsensical quagmires of conceptual confusions.

I

FAULTY ASSUMPTIONS

If academicians are being honest without mincing words, they would admit the only alternative to explicitly naming and defining an ill-defined life-problem is to basically *guess* its answer. For it is a given that the primary means of academically studying how to answer a question properly is through its literal meaning; an inquiry conducted without *that primary means* constitutes unacademic guesswork or an assumption and an outright assault on the English language.[1]

An assumption is a speculative assertion about the life-problem, which may superficially have some justification. But these few outer layers of explanations fail to substantively, if not to fundamentally, penetrate into the heart of their inquiry. For instance, Baggini asserted but did *not* provide supporting arguments for love as being one of his five values that constitutes life's meaningfulness; he merely assumed it as such, as he did with his other claims about the sources of the meaning of life.[2] This kind of question-begging often goes unnoticed, like a Trojan horse, because we tend to unwittingly privilege popular beliefs as being exempted from philosophical or critical scrutiny. Once these beliefs take hold in even the most intellectual of minds, it is extremely hard to see the life-question as it truly is without unnecessary bias, but I digress.

To be fair, Baggini perhaps reasoned (quietly) that the meaning of life is somehow intrinsically good for the person living according to it, and love, as being likewise good, must contribute to life's meaning.[3] Let us *assume* then, for the sake of argument, that Baggini *privately* reasons as follows. Notwithstanding extreme cases of suffering, if being alive is better than being dead, and meaning is better than meaninglessness, then we must accept that both desiderata are even more preferable while combined.[4]

---

1. If defining a problem were so obviously an academic standard, then why did so many philosophers miss it? As we shall see in chapter 6, there is not a single philosopher who defined 'the meaning of life' properly.

2. First, it is worth restating that the total sources of life's meaning, according to Baggini, is at least six, if we include *aesthetic appreciation* among them. Second, the details about love and whether it must involve someone else, an object, or for someone to love himself are unimportant for the purpose of my illustration.

3. I mean 'good' in the neutral and amoral sense, e.g., the wind is *good* for a forest fire.

4. The same reasoning applies to other sources, such as happiness.

However, there is no support for the beliefs that 'the meaning of life,' under any of its lexical references, must be intrinsically good or strictly entail love as a source of its meaning. David Benatar is the obvious counterexample to the belief that the meaning of life is intrinsically good; he would firstly deny life has any ultimate meaning, and, secondly, even if life were ultimately meaningful, he would deny it as being sufficient for life to be worthwhile *qua* intrinsically good. Benatar titled his book *Better Never to Have Been: The Harm of Coming into Existence* partly after a verse of Sophocles' poem, cited at the beginning of his second chapter:

> Never to have been born is best
> But if we must see the light, the next best
> Is quickly returning whence we came.
> When youth departs, with all its follies,
> Who does not stagger under evils? Who escapes them?[5]

According to Benatar's pleasure-pain calculus, which I shall not elaborate for the sake of brevity, "there is no net benefit to coming into existence and thus coming into existence is never worth its costs."[6] Benatar "allows for death to be a benefit more often than the usual view [common sense]," and he "would claim more suicides to be rational," as opposed to being caused by mental illness.[7] But he ironically stops short of recommending suicide.

Arthur Schopenhauer describes us from our childhood years as "innocent prisoners, condemned, not to death, but to life."[8] He writes, moreover, so as to extend his criticisms to the most privileged lives imaginable:

> If the world were a paradise of luxury and ease, a land
> flowing with milk and honey, where every Jack obtained
> his Jill at once and without any difficulty, men would ei-
> ther die of boredom or hang themselves; or there would
> be wars, massacres, and murders; so that in the end

5. 18.

6. *Better Never*, 13.

7. *Better Never*, 13.

8. "On the Sufferings," 3.

mankind would inflict more suffering on itself than it has
now to accept at the hands of Nature.[9]

Life in every case is not only miserable and full of suffering, according to Schopenhauer, and Benatar, but it also continues to worsen until the day we die, assuming death is truly inevitable. Even if one finds life turned out "tolerably well," Schopenhauer says, "[T]he longer you live the more clearly you feel that, on the whole, life is *a disappointment, nay, a cheat.*"[10]

Life's insufferableness aside, neither Schopenhauer nor Benatar deny that love *could* be a source of life's meaning. Schopenhauer concludes, nevertheless, as Baggini claims, by writing "that which is [*sic.*] after all [*sic.*] the most necessary thing in life—the tolerance, patience, regard, and *love* of neighbour."[11][12] Benatar believes that "[l]ife is meaningless, but it also has meaning—or, more accurately, meanings. . . . One can transcend the self and make a positive mark on the lives of others in myriad ways. These include nurturing and teaching the young, caring for the sick, bringing relief to the suffering . . ." or, in other words, living life meaningfully by propagating acts of *love* for the benefit of society.[13] It is important to note that Benatar's "meanings" of life are "terrestrial" and do not make life meaningful in the "cosmic" or ultimate sense.[14] But in addressing a plural life-problem, even if Benatar were right, *which he is not,* he is addressing a wholly different inquiry as I had

9. Schopenhauer, "On the Sufferings," 2–3.

10. "On the Sufferings," 3.

11. "On the Sufferings," 9; my emphasis.

12. Schopenhauer's comment about "tolerance, patience, regard, and love of neighbour" ironically contrasts a lawsuit in Berlin, for which he was eventually found guilty of assault and battery against his neighbor, Caroline Louise Marquet (Cartwright, *Schopenhauer: A Biography*). While this does not disprove what Schopenhauer wrote about treating others with warmth and respect, it calls into question his sincerity. The truth of this incident with his neighbor is unknown, as Schopenhauer denies using excessive force. However, he does admit to calling her an old wretch, which he regretted in *Gesammelte Briefe* (Schopenhauer).

13. *The Human Predicament,* 63

14. *The Human Predicament,* 62–3

shown through the use of linguistics, throughout chapter 2. This means it has no bearing on the original problem of meaning, so I shall not delve further into Benatar's theory of life.

I now turn my attention to a counterexample against the second belief about love being a source of the meaning of life. This shall require some elaboration because it comes in the form of an allegorical anecdote.

In an old Eastern fable recalled by Tolstoy, a traveler finds himself pursued by a deadly beast. To escape being mauled to death, he jumps into a well and, to avoid plunging to his death, grasps a branch of a bush protruding from a crevice within the well's bricky wall. Beneath him lies a fearsome dragon with its mouth wide-open as it anticipates its delectable guest. The traveler cannot climb his way out, for the deadly beast awaits an easy meal, but the behemoth beneath him likewise hungers. His arms grow increasingly tired from clutching the bush's branch, and, worse, two mice, one black and the other white, begin chewing away at the branch, assuring the traveler of his impending demise. Before the branch could give way, the traveler notices honey oozing from the bush's leaves and stretches out his tongue for a last taste of sweetness before he perishes. Two drops of honey fall, and Tolstoy writes of himself, "I try to suck the honey that once consoled me, but the honey is no longer sweet."[15].

The mice and their symbolic shades of white and black signify 'day' and 'night,' respectively, and the traveler's fixation on them is Tolstoy's growing obsession with death, as his remaining days of life dwindle. Toward the middle of the fable, the traveler returns his gaze to the dragon; Tolstoy explains the fearsome behemoth represents "the terrible truth," which is the *inevitability of death*. He describes each drop of honey that once consoled him as representing "my love for my family and my writing."[16] But in contrast to Baggini's buoyant conclusion, which we saw in chapter 2 includes happiness, Tolstoy pithily ended the fable by calling the "happiness

15. *Confession*, 31.
16. Tolstoy, *Confession*, 31.

of life" a "delusion" that no longer "deceives" him.[17] Tolstoy then declared that "[e]verything else [apart from the terrible truth] is a lie."[18] The "delusion" he mentioned includes his love for his wife and thirteen children, which ceased to comfort him inasmuch as it lost its sweetness. For Tolstoy, love and all things non-divine simply cannot give life meaning without God, and one's belief in God's existence; if life and all things human and humanly achievable are destructible and ephemeral (in a godless universe), then he thinks one may as well avoid unnecessarily futile and lifelong struggles by committing suicide.

Although neither counterexample disproves the meaning of life as being intrinsically good and love as one of its sources, Benatar's, Schopenhauer's, and Tolstoy's world-famous writings make it clear that the beliefs do not go unchallenged. The difference between the former three thinkers and Baggini is that the former *provided* reasons to justify their controversial claims without ever presuming readers would agree with them every step along the way. Whereas Baggini possibly believed love's desirability so obvious that it required no justification. This was a gross omission by Baggini given how well-known Tolstoy is and that his book denies that love is neither necessary nor sufficient for the meaning of life. By default, the reasons Benatar, Schopenhauer, and Tolstoy provided for their views, as opposed to Baggini's silence, would therefore give them an upper hand over Baggini. But I shall not elaborate on any of their arguments, since even if we assume the truths of their premises, provided they pertain to the meaning of life, their conclusions still do not follow. In other words, Benatar, Schopenhauer, and Tolstoy are guilty of non-sequiturs, and I shall later revisit Tolstoy's journey to find God and the meaning of life. As for now, these views are, as a whole, besides the point I am proving, and I favor none among them. Rather, the purpose of my illustrations is how, in the absence of pertinent facts, pairs of mutually contradictory assumptions could be argued to a *stalemate*. That is, if we were to assume that Baggini, in response to Tolstoy,

17. *Confession*, 31.
18. *Confession*, 31.

bolstered his claims about the meaning of life; this would require Baggini to explain why he is justified in choosing his sources of meaning in the place of other claims, including Tolstoy's claim about finding God. But I am not obligated to do Baggini's work for him unless he includes me as a paid coauthor for a possible revision of his book.

To borrow David Hume's phrase, unless Baggini establishes a "necessary connexion" between life's meaning or purpose and love, then it is perennially dubitable whether love, rather than its exact opposite, is truly relevant. (And the same is true of all other fundamentally unjustified claims.) One may argue with equal plausibility that apathy and not love is what life signifies or has for its end; after all, 'meaning' and 'purpose' do not necessarily imply something desirable or "good." For instance, Schopenhauer believes that the boredom following one's fulfillment of desires, which happens to be a form of apathy, plays a large part in the abundance of misery and suffering throughout life. Schopenhauer wrote elsewhere, "[I]t would accordingly be more correct to put the purpose of life in our woe than in welfare."[19] By "woe," Schopenhauer means *any* form of suffering, including the state of *boredom* occurring while one is undistracted by the evanescent thrills of pursuing desires. He says, "[T]he more one suffers, the sooner is the true end of life attained, and that the more happily one lives, the more is that end postponed."[20] And, as demonstrated in the previous chapter, Baggini *did* equivocate between "meaning" in 'the meaning of life' with 'purpose.' So, this would place Schopenhauer's view of life's purpose as the direct antithesis of Baggini's theory of life, especially with respect to happiness. Therefore, if love leads to happiness, then Schopenhauer would consider it incongruent with the purpose of life (or what Baggini indiscriminately calls "the meaning of life"). With so many mutually exclusive assumptions, such as theist *contra* secular theories of life, there would be no end to

19. *Will and Representation*, vol. 2: 635.

20. Schopenhauer, *Will and Representation*, vol. 2: 635.

second-guessing any one of them as being true of *the* meaningful or purposeful life.[21]

It is worth noting that the aforementioned "necessary connexion" would have to be an analytic truth, such as the relationship between a symbol and its meaning, e.g., ''8' is a number.' Analytic statements *cannot* fail to be true, and the denial of any one of them always results in a self-contradiction. Whereas empirical statements, e.g., 'There are eight planets in the Solar System,' lack absolute certainty, and they are contingent and highly probable of being true in the best-case scenario. For example, the number of planets may change once again, as it did from nine planets in August 2006. For instance, Pluto's erstwhile status as a planet could be reinstated, new Solar System planets could be discovered, or a planet other than the Earth could be swallowed whole by the Sun and destroyed.[22] Therefore, analytic truths outrank empirical facts in terms of certainty; observable facts are vulnerable to pervasive skepticism, whereas analytic truths, if formulated properly, are indubitable.[23] For example, if the analytic proposition ''8' is a number.' is a number' lacks ambiguity with the help of proper context, then a competent skeptic cannot doubt the truth of what lacks any possibility of being false. Either way, both analytic truths and facts are more justified than assumptions, provided that they are *relevant*. Neither Baggini nor Benatar nor Schopenhauer nor Tolstoy provided either relevant analytic truths or, at the very least, pertinent facts to support their most fundamental claims about

21. The same applies to the other sources of meanings Baggini claimed as the meaning of life, including what I previously distinguished as being of significance rather than value or worthwhile purpose, i.e., aesthetics or the appreciation of pleasure.

22. I say "a planet other than the Earth" because if our beloved home planet is destroyed, then there would be no humans to officially declare as fact the new number of planets in the Solar System. But if, in the event of the Earth's destruction, the International Space Station or its equivalent were somehow left untouched, the few survivors remaining would have much more pressing concerns than accounting for the number of Solar System planets.

23. I shall address some of the cleverer objections against analytic truths in chapters 5–6, but doing so here only distracts readers from my intentions within this chapter.

life's meaning. Ergo, none of the thinkers' views mentioned is more credible on a fundamental or substantive level than those of the others.

With what I have covered about assumptions in mind, any admission of guesswork by my adversaries would prove self-defeating; it would place them in the embarrassing position of explaining why they insist on rejecting linguistics as a proven method for problem-solving while espousing speculation in its stead. *If* philosophers could ever agree on a single thing, it is that speculation almost never works—their denial of *this* would ironically prove my point—and whenever it does, its success cannot be explained; it cannot be the basis for a real theory because its results are neither replicable nor generalizable, and so the contents of speculative claims cannot be *demonstrated*. It is, therefore, understandable why philosophers of life seldom term their own claims "guesses" or "assumptions," as such intellectually humble words of contrition are perceived or used as the philosophy equivalent of profanities. In truth, theorists are *obligated* to explicitly state their assumptions as such whenever they make them, without embellishing their unsubstantiated or unjustified claims with closely accompanied words such as 'surely,' 'certainly,' 'obviously,' etc.

II

THEORY-CRIPPLING STALEMATES

While a lack of foundational justification and the uncertainty of a speculative claim are not theory-crippling *per se*, the stalemates ensuing from a preponderance of rivaling and mutually exclusive assumptions certainly are. For the sake of clarity, unjustified and unsubstantiated assumptions are of the same nature, i.e., they are unfounded claims. Stalemates defeat the ultimate purpose of inquiring because an inquiry that leads nowhere is futile. Speculative philosophy is akin to firing a machine gun in random directions at an unknown target in pitch-black darkness.[24] Should any un-

24. Should one counter my example with the mordaciously sarcastic

founded assumption miraculously strike its "intended" target, no one would know of its success for certain or why it "succeeded." Philosophy must lead somewhere through *gainful* discourse. But even while those who disagree with me may think it sufficient that philosophy is conducted for its own sake, the blind acceptance of aimless speculation is not philosophy proper; it is an academic blunder with faulty reasoning and amounts to pseudo-philosophy and grandiloquent nonsense for the sake of evading criticism and is, thus, indistinguishable from the crudely expressed opinions of the vulgar masses.

The impasse of furthering an inquiry is caused by the indeterminate truth-value possessed by each assumption or unjustified claim. An indeterminate truth-value occurs whenever a proposition's claim asserts something that is neither observable nor denoted in the literal meaning of symbols, such as words and numbers. So, a truth-indeterminate claim cannot be proved or disproved, or true or false. For example, it is impossible to "observe" the relationship between love and the meaning of life, and love is not denoted or analytically contained within the life-phrase thereof. Such an indeterminate claim is unlike the empirical statement 'there are eight planets in the Solar System' or the analytic statement ''8' is a number.' As of *now*, few assumptions about the meaning of life are refutable, since their rebuttals are likewise truth-indeterminate assumptions. Truth-indeterminate claims cannot confirm or confute other truth-indeterminate claims for the same reason adding or subtracting '0' from any number neither increases nor decreases its value.[25] Philosophy of life's decadent literature is an ironic departure from David Hume's conclusion in *An Enquiry Concerning Human Understanding*:

---

suggestion of flicking on a light switch before firing in pitch-black darkness, I would add that the light switch in question represents "defining a problem." My counter-sarcasm is more effective. For once the problem is well-defined, then we actually *know* what we are trying to solve. So, this rebuttal would have no effect but to further prove the need for linguistics, which is the example's equivalent of flicking on a light switch.

25. For those seeking to challenge my example: I am speaking of arithmetic operations *only* and not other possible uses of '0.'

> When we run over libraries, persuaded of these prin-
> ciples, what havoc must we make? If we take in our
> hand any volume; of divinity or school metaphysics, for
> instance; let us ask, *Does it contain any abstract reason-
> ing concerning quantity or number?* No. *Does it contain
> any experimental reasoning concerning matter of fact and
> existence?* No. Commit it then to the flames: for it can
> contain nothing but sophistry and illusion.[26]

Hume's mention of "abstract reasoning concerning quantity or number" and "experimental reasoning" are different words to express what he elsewhere calls "relations of ideas" and "matters of facts"; today, we know them as 'analytic truths' and 'facts' or, for the unlearned, 'abstract' and 'concrete,' respectively. Indeterminacies are effectively nil-valued and uninformative because they are neither analytic nor factual, and neither do they hold any heuristic use other than being an example of fallacious reasoning and how not to repeat fallacies. While it would be a shame to *incinerate* what may still prove educational, ornamental, or amusing in posterity, Hume is right about dismissing pseudo-academic writings, which amount to nothing but sophistry and illusion. If any progress toward the meaning of life should be attained, the obfuscation of metaphysical debris must be cleared by jettisoning nonsensical claims. That is, figuratively speaking, unless one is comfortable conversing through the cacophony of mind-numbing nightclub music or a cafeteria full of effervescently disputatious schoolchildren.

A tie-breaker or a claim's refutation, then, must involve a positive element of value from either a *relevant* field of expertise, analytic truths, or both. For instance, if 'meaning' is immaterial, then it would not follow, as it would be irrelevant to argue through *physical* facts, that "life is meaningless." As I had previously stated against Cottingham, the physical sciences are not the only kind of science. For all that is currently known about the meaning of life, its answer could very well be a collection of abstractions and not objects "in" the world. The lack of any *intelligible* explanation

26. 176.

for this "meaning" that philosophers thoughtlessly insist as being of one category, rather than another, does not make it so. For instance, William Lane Craig's claim that "life itself is absurd" and "without ultimate significance, value, or purpose" because "there will be no heat"[27] or a Heat Death is suspiciously non-sequitur on its own. It is possible, after all, that 'meaning' is independent of the second law of thermodynamics and from our mortality in a godless universe. So, the ambiguity provides an additional reason the meaning of life *needs* the use of linguistics. Only then, when we understand the true meaning of those key words, e.g., 'meaning' and 'life,' which philosophers unsparingly use with carelessness, will we be able to learn whether life is absurd or not.

Once the strict, literal interpretation of a life-problem loses priority over speculation, the last and only academic means to intellectually *compel* agreement between philosophers, with an ounce of intellectual honesty and humility, is forgone. Without relevant facts and analytic truths, the baseless and irrelevant claims, which do not self-contradict, are neither provable nor refutable. This means philosophers will always—for eternity if time permitted—argue against the same old theories time and time again, as they did for over two and a half millennia. As for the claims that self-contradict: they are self-evidently impossible and cancel themselves out because their value is negative (i.e., false) and not nil-valued. So, unlike desultory assumptions, which are far worse perennial nuisances because they do not self-contradict, impossibilities have a determinate truth-value as being always false, thankfully, and, thus, they are the least of our worries.

A claim that lacks a determinate truth-value is neither more nor less probable of being true than another claim that is likewise unsubstantiated by facts and unsupported by analytic truths. Truth-indeterminate claims are incapable of being impossible, unlikely, probable, or indubitable because they are nil-valued and *inert*. They are analogous to the nonsensical or empty statement I previously quoted from Chomsky, i.e., "Colorless green ideas sleep

27. "Absurdity of Life," 41.

furiously."[28] To be clear, the theoretical implication of presumptive claims *being truth-indeterminate* is insufficient to refute them until they are compared to the answer to the meaning of life, which has yet to be known; they are, for the time being, as irrefutable as the Homeric Gods. However, the inability of truth-indeterminate assumptions to break stalemates obviates their feasibility as answers worth their ink, much less as academically worthy answers to the meaning of life. Assumptions come cheaply, and there are no limits to how many that could be made about the meaning of life save one's imagination.

In a fact-barren stalemate, there could never be a non-contrived "winner," or a comparatively "better" assumption, or any "worthwhile" collaboration. Speculative philosophy is, instead, a mere popularity contest, whose verdict of what is most "plausible" or "intuitive" depends on how obsequiously well a "theory" reaffirms commonly held biases and the trends of specious sentiments. In any case, the theory that fails to genuinely advance the philosophy of life is effectively a loser.

III

THE GOD-EXPLANATION

One quick-and-easy response to the inconvenience of stalemates is for a philosopher of life to unnecessarily insert what is befittingly termed a 'god-explanation.' As this chapter's title indicates, 'Deus ex Machina' is Latin for 'god from the machine,' which I borrow from one of Plato's dialogues. In *Cratylus*, Socrates was critical of tragic poets who were sudden in introducing overly convenient plot devices for escaping perplexity.[29] Likewise, theist philosophers of various religions are guilty of divining a contrived "explanation" they believe capable of shouldering the problem-solving burdens for them. But as we shall see, even if the deity in question exists, we

28. *Syntactic Structures*, 15.
29. *Complete Works*, 425e.

would still be nowhere closer to solving the meaning of life, other than merely knowing its answer is *possible.*

The various strategies employed by theist philosophers draw their impetus by exploiting their readers' deep-seated vanities and fears, rather than the coolness of reason with conclusions whose truths follow their premises' truths. For instance, Craig, and Cottingham rebut secular explanations of life's meaning by likening humans to unsavory insects and animals in a godless world. Craig writes, "Mankind is thus no more significant than a swarm of mosquitos or a barnyard of pigs, for their end is all the same."[30] And Cottingham, who seems more eager than the former in drawing self-degrading comparisons, repeats several times Blaise Pascal's contemptuous description of us as being "imbecile worms."[31] But we must ask ourselves: does Craig's colorful and potentially unpalatable comparisons between humans and "mosquitoes," "pigs," "dogs," "rats," "guinea pigs," or a bitter Pascal's "imbecile worms" demonstrate that some god or another exists? To spell out the obvious answer: no, it does not. Any philosopher worth his professional prefix knows these are not *valid* arguments for any god's existence.

If we think carefully about what potential assumptions underlie the comparison between humans and "lowly" creatures, the vain wish for wanting a special place in an indifferent universe is not an argument for theism; it would amount to no more than an appeal to subjectivity. In effect, the kindred comparisons propagated by theists only succeeded in encouraging irreligious thinkers, such as John Gray, to declare that "[h]uman life has no more meaning than the life of slime mould."[32] At worst, these theist claims, likening human beings to "lowly" creatures, are ineffectual. For instance, secular thinkers like Richard Taylor openly embraced the human-worm comparison by finding all forms of life significant in their own way; as we had previously seen, he believes the meaning is "from within" and not "without." Taylor

30. "Absurdity of Life," 42.

31. *On the Meaning,* 33, 33 (footnote 6), and 35.

32. Gray, *Straw Dogs,* 33.

writes, moreover, "[T]he result is going to be exactly the same," whether we look at the life-cycle of an "ugly worm" in the caves of New Zealand or that of any human.[33] The Sisyphean life-cycle of cave worms hatching, feeding, cocooning, flying, mating, and dying is ultimately the same with humans; it had been "going on for millions of years, [sic.] and to no end other than that the same meaningless cycle may continue for another millions [sic.] of years."[34] In any case, whether the churlish comparisons hold or not (i.e., those drawn by Craig, and Cottingham in their *ex hypothesi* godless world), they are non-sequitur. Even if we do not want to be as insignificant as worms or be likened to pigs, it does not follow that one deity or another must exist for life to have meaning. Neither is it truly a problem whether the life of a worm is as meaningful as that of a human, lest our self-esteem is as pathetically fragile and vain as theists had hoped.

Let us put to rest our narcissistic tendencies for aspiring to be the center of the universe and turn to the more pressing problem of suicide. Does it follow from a godless universe that we may as well avoid unnecessary struggles and suffering by ending our lives, assuming that everything involving our existence is destructible and temporary? As Tolstoy explained of his suicidal past, "Rational knowledge led me to the conclusion that life is meaningless; my life came to a halt, and I wanted to do away with myself."[35][36] It is true that "rational knowledge," as consisting of all of our sciences, whether physical, e.g., chemistry, or abstract, e.g., Euclidean geometry, cannot *justify* continued life. But even as the choice of whether to end life or continue living is essentially a matter of preference in a godless universe, the problem of suicide is irrelevant to the meaning of life. The sudden realization, if any, that life has meaning is unlikely to make a difference to a suicidally depressed person. Suicide is an issue best left to the study of mental health

33. "The Meaning of Life," 170.

34. Taylor, "The Meaning of Life," 171.

35. *Confession*, 60.

36. "Rational knowledge" is Tolstoy's reference to Descartes, and he makes no secret of being influenced by him.

and a supportive family; it may be prevented by a change in habits, a new purpose, a change in circumstances, and perhaps psychotherapy. In any case, if a person struggles with suicidal depression, his submission to the God of Craig, or Cottingham, or even Lovecraft's Cthulhu would only put off one's own problems until they resurface again. For instance, long after Tolstoy found "the meaning of life" through God in *Confession*, he lived so miserably with his wife that he fled his home and died of pneumonia days later.[37]

But enough about the peripheral issues concerning the consequences of a godless universe; what of a world with a god? Would our acknowledgment of the existence of a god as powerful and benevolent as Craig's be sufficient to finally solve the meaning of life? Alternatively, could a philosopher's introduction of Cthulhu, Allah, Yahweh, Krishna, or any supreme being to the philosophy of life "fix" the problem of life's meaning? John Kekes flips these questions on their heads: "If the meaning of life depends on understanding and being motivated to live according to a cosmic order, then life has no meaning because we cannot understand the cosmic order and consequently cannot be motivated by it."[38] A world with the corresponding god(s) of any religion would still be insufficient for explaining why Hindu, Jewish, Christian, or Muslim traditions are more meaning-conferring to life than binge drinking or collecting bottle caps. The insertion of a god-explanation would be as uninteresting and uninformative an answer to the meaning of life as attributing the Big Bang as the cause of a particular car or tree; if I want to know whether a car is a Rolls-Royce or whether a colossal tree is an oak, a superlative answer like the Big Bang-explanation would not be an answer worth taking seriously. It would leave us none the wiser—it would tell us absolutely nothing—about certain things we would like to know about a particular car or tree.[39] Essentially, superlative explanations are useless and dissatisfying because they could be attributed to anything

37. Tchertkoff, *Last Days*.

38. "The Meaning of Life," 24.

39. To be clear, the "car" or "tree" we would "like to know about" is analogous to the meaning of life.

without explaining anything. Whether the universe began with a bang, was created by a supreme and intelligent being, or has always existed, the meaning of life requires more than a facile, superlative answer to be intellectually satisfying; it requires a real, non-lazy, serious, and fundamentally justified answer. Tolstoy, Craig, and Cottingham have not demonstrated how God solves the meaning of life; they have merely asserted that their God causes life to be possibly meaningful. For it is one thing to say life is meaningful and another to demonstrate why and how life is meaningful in the way two and two equals four.

In short, the mysteriousness of gods and religions in theistic theories of life renders them far too vague and devoid of facts to be demonstrable; it says *literally* nothing about everything denoted by 'the meaning of life,' except, perhaps, that some god or another, or many gods, caused, permitted, or declared life to be meaningful. Theism is irrelevant insofar as it is too general to provide an interesting answer (i.e., something informative) to the meaning of life, other than blackmailing those refusing to believe it with nihilism and despair. Problem-solving is not a task that could be delegated to a god, even if the god in question exists; if we should have any hope of ever solving the meaning of life, the hard, intellectual labor has to actually be done by a real person.

IV

CONCLUSION

Although many readers may express displeasure with my unelaborate and unadorned dismissal of theism, they may find comfort in knowing that I had not followed Baggini, and Kekes in rejecting any religion as false. Like other truth-indeterminate claims, many religious claims are neither true nor false. I was not about to increase the length of my book by an additional 100 pages to reject as irrelevant what could be stated in fewer words. But even in supposing the existence of Craig's Abrahamic God, we predictably came nowhere closer to solving the meaning of life. These superlative answers are incapable of providing ones that are definite and quantifiable as we so often see with any real science, true propositions, or anything slightly informative. Even with abstractions such as the arithmetic operation '2 + 2 = 4,' we are able to unequivocally know its components with certainty, and, yet, like any god, they are not physically observable. For instance, we know that the sum '4' results from two variables, i.e., the addend and augend, and the plus sign. Whereas a god-explanation does little else but assert the truth of one deity over another and the need of performing certain religious rituals; it tells us nothing definite and interesting about the meaning of life. The whole purpose of inquiring about the meaning of life is to find its answer, and it must be demonstrable. A theory of life that is deserving of its ink must be able to explain its claims definitively and without any air of mysteriousness and hocus-pocus.

Since theism is by far the most believed worldview among laypeople to this day, the issue involving religions, gods, and the meaning of life was inevitably bound to arise. In the year I wrote this book, the three major branches of Abrahamic religions combined rule the beliefs, minds, and lives of over half the world's population. As a recurring theme in the philosophy of life and one of the greatest sources of conceptual confusions, fallacies, and mysterious god-explanations, theistic theories of life cannot be left unscrutinized. And as the single greatest source of stalemates, thanks to secularists' and theists' urge to argue about religion among themselves in a field that does not seem to be about theism, there could not be a more suitable example than the belief in the supernatural to illustrate these philosopher-made problems.[40]

It is worth mentioning that the dismissal of one major kind of view in the philosophy of life must not be a cause for concern; no progress in solving the meaning of life was lost, since religion-based theories had never managed to explain anything new and informative about the meaning of life. Instead, the departure of

---

40. Should I be accused of playing favorites, it should be known that I already criticized atheism for likewise introducing truth-indeterminate claims to the philosophy of life in the first chapter.

theism as the meaning of life's explanation means one less competing view and one less mind-numbing song in a nightclub's playlist or one less schoolchild disrupting gainful, philosophical discourse. With one less alternative to my linguistic method (i.e., naming and defining a problem), we draw nearer to its truth, as there are now fewer obstacles to solving the meaning of life. However, before turning to the much-sought answer to the meaning of life, there still remains subjectivism, pseudo-objectivism, and hybrids of the theories thereof, which, as alternatives to my own, must be displaced.[41]

I shall revisit language in chapter 5 and apply linguistics and some logic in chapter 6 to solve the meaning of life.

41. Although stronger forms of subjectivism lack proponents, we cannot wait until a philosopher eventually decides to adopt them; subjectivism, in all its forms, must be addressed as they invite the perennial problem of relativism, which would obfuscate solving life-problems as theism once had.

Aside from subjectivism, the so-called "objective" theories of life are more appropriately 'pseudo-objective,' as they have not been indubitably established as being of objective meaning; this shall be discussed in chapter 4.

Chapter 4

Colorizing Absurdity

IN THIS CHAPTER, I shall dismantle all theories of life purporting to address 'the meaning of life' before introducing my very own. This begins with exposing subjectivism as entailing multiple perennial problems. I shall likewise extend these issues to involve all other contemporary theories of life, including putatively "objective" theories. Since the philosophy-of-life inquiries are numerous and diverse, any further reference to 'theories of life' and 'the philosophy of life' (unless stated otherwise) shall only imply writings pertaining to the meaning of life.

My general argument herein makes three mutually supporting claims. First, contemporary theories of life are unable to prevent the philosophy of life from descending into radical relativism for reasons seen in chapter 3; to be explicit, I am referring to truth-indeterminate propositions and stalemates as being the causes of relativism. Second, if radical relativism is the case, then life neither has an objective nor intersubjective meaning; this is evidenced by the complete lack of pertinent facts and relevant analytic truths in the philosophy of life as of *now*. Thus, the successful argument for radical relativism entails by its own nature nihilism. I shall not bother, until chapter 6, to further elaborate on nihilism insofar as it is, by default, the absence of objective meaning, so its practical and philosophical implications are fairly obvious. But most importantly, I want my readers to keep in mind that theories unable to surmount radical relativism also face nihilism and, wherever "objective" or "non-subjective" claims are dubitable, skepticism as well. By the end of this chapter, it shall become clear that, third, to avoid the compounded fate all contemporary theories of life share, philosophers must stop ignoring or grossly underestimating linguistics. That is, unless they are comfortable with the philosophy of life's usual state of affairs, which involves all progress concerning the life-problems suspended as the result of pointless speculations and endless stalemates.

The act of philosophizing must, after all, lead *somewhere*, and naming and defining the *problem* (i.e., 'the meaning of life') is part of how to avoid the aforementioned, perennial problems (e.g., skepticism).

I

SUBJECTIVISM AND PERSPECTIVAL RELATIVISM

Perspectival relativism (henceforth 'relativism') is the claim that different individuals may have different attitudes, feelings, beliefs, opinions, interpretations, or, as I prefer, *perspectives* about the meaning of life. With few exceptions, relativism further claims that each person cannot be wrong about their perspectives.[1] For

1. The "exceptions" thereof depend on the relativist and whether he denies moral or logical principles or whether certain sciences are reducible to being mere perspectives. The relativist may thus disqualify subjective views that contradict certain principles or facts from being privileged as perspectives. But whether the relativist is successful or not at doing so is quite arguable.

On a separate note, there is an *intrapersonal* aspect (i.e., from within) of subjectivism, which is worthy of mention. A person's interpretations about life-problems most likely change many times throughout his lifetime, but I shall not draw upon this issue outside of this footnote, as it is unnecessary for establishing radical relativism.

This aforementioned intrapersonal issue carries a risk for a relativist's theory; if the relativist chooses to favor (by declaring true) a person's perspectives at one point in time rather than another, then the relativist risks collapsing relativism into a non-relativistic theory of non-subjective truth. Alternatively, the relativist may presume that we are different persons from moment to moment and treat all of a person's conflicting views at different points of his life as being equally privileged.

example, one person may view the meaning of life as "gloomy," and another may see it as "cheerful," but neither view is false even if they mutually contradict; the truth-value between different persons' views is incommensurable because there is no mind-independent truth-maker for judging perspectives (that is known as of now).[2] For instance, the meaning of life, according to Jones, cannot be evaluated according to Smith's perspective, and, likewise, Smith's answer to the meaning of life cannot be judged according to the perspective of Jones. Whereas subjectivism focuses purely on the intrapersonal aspect of a perspective with respect to the meaning of life, relativism involves both the intrapersonal *and* the interpersonal aspects.

Depending on the subjective theorist, subjectivism gives an individual varying authority to determine for himself the meaning of life, and perspectival relativism is the belief that all individuals' perspectives are veridically equal; that is, insofar as there are no non-subjective means to meaningfully judge perspectives. The purer and less substantive the subjectivist view is, the more authority an individual has over determining the, or, rather, *their* answer to the meaning of life. In this respect, subjectivism would usually allow each subject to become the near-indisputable truth-maker of their own perspectives.

Relativism claims perspectives are *privileged* from being judged false, and that is implicitly based on the belief that there are no non-subjective means for evaluating a perspective outside of a subject's point of view.[3] So, by this implicit token, any judgment rendered about a particular belief would carry equal epistemic weight to the belief being judged, since the former is as much a perspective as the latter. For example, the propositions 'the meaning of life is gloomy' and 'the meaning of life is not gloomy' are both true, but their truth must only correspond to different

2. I intentionally used the descriptions "gloomy" and "cheerful" to de-emphasize the perspective itself and emphasize the *radical* extent to which a relativist is willing to privilege a person's perception about the meaning of life.

3. If there are *absolute* and *known* objective means for judging statements about the meaning of life, then there would be no room for interpreting it subjectively, and, thus, relativism would be false and impossible.

persons holding either belief exclusively. If one person holds both beliefs *simultaneously*, then the relativist may either treat one or both beliefs as being non-perspectives and remove their epistemic privilege; explain the individual as being two "different" persons in a single body with differing beliefs, e.g., someone with disassociative identity disorder, which is otherwise known as multiple personality disorder, or, simply, the individual is conflicted and did not yet decide what he truly believes or changes his mind easily. The first two responses to the contradiction seem less believable than the third since it is not uncommon for a person to be unsure of what he wants to believe or to change his mind easily. As for the aforementioned propositions being held separately by two different individuals, relativism claims they cannot contradict insofar as they are incommensurable; each perspective-fueled proposition is true in virtue of its corresponding individual (the embodied truth-maker) believing it, so it is true for him while being neither true nor false with respect to another person.

Although subjectivism and relativism are evidently not the same theory, the claims they make are not always independent, but it is possible that all claims by both theories are ultimately interdependent; any claim about perspectives on the part of *perspectival* relativism *presupposes* the subjects of subjectivism to whom these perspectives belong. So, perspectival relativism always presupposes subjectivism (but it is unclear if the converse applies). This means that if subjectivism is not the case for the meaning of life, then neither is relativism; relativism requires, firstly, subjects who are capable of perspectives and beliefs and, secondly, that there are no non-subjective truths concerning the meaning of life. Moreover, the dependency between relativism and subjectivism is determined by how much authority a subjective theorist is willing to ascribe to subjects; if there is too little authority granted to subjects in a subjectivist theory, then there may not be room for relativism. However, I shall eventually argue that *all* subjectivist theories are doomed to entail relativism because the constraints to a subject's authority are either arbitrary and indefensible or vulnerable to skepticism.[4]

If the subjectivism in question is a *hybrid* theory, which *includes* objective or non-subjective elements, then the theory thereof is making an implicit denial of relativism. For example, these "objective elements" may constrain or disqualify selfish, destructive, self-destructive, or pointless perspectives from contributing meaningfully to the life of the person to whom these perspectives belong. Thus, a hybrid subjectivist theory grants each subject less authority or freedom than a purer subjectivist theory to determine what they believe is the meaning of life. For instance, the infamous subjectivist, Richard Taylor, claims that "endless activity, which gets nowhere, is just what it is [i.e.] their [a person's] will to pursue. This is its [life's] whole justification and meaning," but adds shortly after, "The point of his [a human being] living is simply to be living."[5] This last point is crucial for Taylor, as it appears he is implicitly trying to exclude from his brand of subjectivism views or pursuits that contribute to self-destruction, e.g., suicide. As being a non-negotiable criterion or one independent of the privileged subjective perspective, Taylor's subjectivism is therefore a hybrid with a *prima facie* non-subjective requirement rather than a theory implicitly coupled with relativism.

However, the coupling of subjectivism with non-subjective elements, criteria, or requirements does not always preclude relativism. For example, it is arguable whether the espousal of objective or non-subjective elements from logical principles makes a subjectivist theory non-relativistic, since logic is necessary for all theories to remain intelligible, coherent, and viable. If a perspective violates the law of non-contradiction or the law of identity from an *intrapersonal* aspect, then even under relativism, it may lose its privilege as being true of its corresponding person; if a

---

4. When I say "arbitrary and indefensible," I mean that a stipulation made by a theorist fails to establish itself as being non-subjective; whereas a stipulation that is "vulnerable to skepticism" does seem to possess some justification, but its truth is not indubitable and thus subject to a skeptic's doubt.

5. "The Meaning of Life," 174.

subject perceives that *the meaning of life is not the meaning of life*, then, assuming both mentions of "the meaning of life" are identical in meaning, that "perspective" cannot fail to be false. Thus, the previously mentioned "belief" is impossible. For even if we assume a person's perspective is privileged and exempted from every criterion imaginable, a self-contradiction or violation of the law of identity prevents that perspective from meaning anything, even subjectively; the individual, to whom the self-contradicting perspective belongs, would not be able to make sense of it for himself, even while relativism aspires to privilege all perspectives. If it does not make sense to its perceiver, then it would be no different than a cacophony, moan, scream, cry, or any incoherent thought, which literally cannot be described as being a 'perspective' anyway. Ergo, a person cannot sincerely believe in a patent contradiction while aware of it, and neither could such a thought qualify as a 'perspective.'[6] Therefore, it is possible for a subjectivist theory to maintain few non-subjective requirements, such as logical principles, and still entail relativism; after all, some intratheoretical coherence is necessary for theories to maintain the minimum level of explanatory intelligibility and potency to qualify as a 'theory,' including relativism.

Logic principles aside, a subjective theory's espousal of other non-subjective elements, such as moral qualifiers or constraints for life to be meaningful, still risks collapsing it into relativism. If a hybrid theory of subjectivism recommends one moral theory in the place of another, for example, a relativist could reduce that

6. Self-contradicting statements, e.g., 'the meaning of life is not the meaning of life,' cannot qualify as perspectives and must be discarded as irrelevant. If a relativist were to insist a self-contradicting statement pertains to the meaning of life, it renders it indiscernible from other, distinct phrases, statements, or questions; for example, if the aforementioned self-contradicting perspective is allowed, then there is nothing preventing "what is the meaning of life?" from becoming indistinguishable from "is the cat on the mat?" Thus, a perspective purporting to be about the meaning of life, while violating a logical principle, falls beyond the scope of my book because it is technically not about the problem thereof. However, in the following sections of this chapter, and in chapter 5, I shall examine the blurred boundaries of 'the meaning of life' under a different context.

non-subjective, moral constraint as being a perspective among other moral perspectives. (But the same reduction cannot apply to logic principles, since, unlike moral theories, if the reader recalls, they are *necessary* for all theories, lest they should self-contradict; without logical principles, there cannot be a theory of anything.) The example of a relativist's reduction of a moral view to a perspective functions similarly to how skepticism raises doubts against any dubitable, non-subjective proposition. While dubitable claims leave enough room for skepticism, they also enable relativists to use skepticism against the possibilities of there being non-subjective or objective answers to the meaning of life. So, the problem of skepticism may compound with relativism in addition to the latter entailing nihilism, i.e., the absence of objective answers to the meaning of life. As the result of the combined relativist and skeptic reasonings, skepticism *cum* relativism are able to establish themselves even while there *are* non-subjective truths, provided that all such truths are dubitable or unknown.

Subjectivists often believe that they could harmonize or reconcile objective or non-subjective claims with subjective beliefs, and this includes the converse, where objectivists espouse some subjective claims, e.g., Susan Wolf in section III. But the view that objective and subjective claims could be harmonized is incompatible for the following analytic reasons. If an answer is truly subjective, it is because it has no true answer other than what a subject truly believes *per se*. However, if an answer is partially non-subjective and its non-subjective portion is true, then including the answer's subjective portion becomes redundant and unnecessary, even if the latter portion does not contradict the former.[7]

My earlier example of criteria excluding selfish, destructive, self-destructive, or pointless perspectives tells us what the meaning of life *is not*, whereas a subjective claim may tell us what it *is*. But in telling what the answer to the meaning of life is not, non-subjective criteria must likewise be able to tell what the problem thereof is. For example, we cannot tell whether an unknown thing is not a circle unless we know, at least, something non-subjective

---

7. I am implying Occam's Razor.

about the thing in question; if the thing in question is a square, then we would certainly know, by definition, it is not a circle.

In stipulating what the meaning of life is not, the hybrid subjectivist is begging the question by presuming to know what has yet to be determined. To make non-subjective stipulations, the subjectivist must have a *non-subjectively true* idea of what the meaning of life is. But since philosophers of life are at a loss as to what *truly* is the answer to the meaning of life, they cannot tell whether these "non-subjective" elements, criteria, or requirements are indeed non-subjective; for what little is currently known of the meaning of life, these "non-subjective" stipulations may very well be mere perspectives expressed by the hybrid subjectivists themselves. Hence, this is why non-subjective elements, criteria, or requirements for claims about the meaning of life are question-begging.

As I wrote near the very beginning of this book, a skeptic only needs a claim to have a single possibility of being false so that he could doubt its truth. Similarly, a single possibility of a claim being perspectival is enough for a relativist to doubt any likelihood the claim is non-subjective; for instance, the assertion that a religion is true—perhaps one that someone grew up believing—and others false is vulnerable to skepticism *cum* relativism. If the hybrid subjectivist should break the spell of skepticism *cum* relativism and prove his stipulated criteria are *indubitably* non-subjective, then he has only succeeded in solving his inquiry non-subjectively. In knowing enough for what the answer to the meaning of life is not, he must know beforehand what it truly is.[8] Therefore, the successful "hybrid subjectivist" theory would actually be an entirely non-subjective theory of life. Ergo, either the meaning of life is determined by the subject, or it is determined non-subjectively, but a "hybrid" theorist cannot have it both ways.

Seeing that the meaning of life is not definitively known as of yet, the "hybrid" theorist cannot be sure whether he is truly stipulating non-subjective criteria or expressing his own perspectives about others' perspectives. Thus, every form of subjectivity cannot

---

8. For those who would insist otherwise: this form of invalid argumentation is known as 'affirming the consequent.'

distance itself from relativism, unless it solves its inquiry while becoming a fully non-subjective theory.

Instead of distancing themselves from relativism, the exasperated subjectivists may opt to go on the offensive, expose relativism's hypocrisy, and refute it by borrowing an argument from one of its staunch critics.[9] If Taylor were to ask the relativist whether 'all claims about the life-problems are perspectives' is itself a perspective, the latter would have no choice but to respond with either a "yes" or "no." (But sometimes the answer could be both a "yes" and "no," as we shall soon see.)

By answering with a "no," the relativist is conceding to Taylor that *at least one* non-subjective truth applies to the meaning of life, i.e., the central claim relativism makes about other views being perspectives. This concession would contradict relativism's implicit or explicit claim about there being *nothing non-subjective* to be said about the meaning of life since relativism's central claim would turn out to be non-subjective. Thus, relativism would self-contradict.

If the relativist answers "yes," then it would appear, in this scenario, relativism fares no better, since, as a perspective, its assertion would carry as little weight as the "perspectives" it judges. So, in this case—as a perspective—relativism's central claim would be in no *credible* (or unarbitrary) position to judge other claims it labels as 'perspectives.' Thus, its central claim would lose its intended effect in treating all the-meaning-of-life claims as equal, since it itself would be equal to other claims, including claims that deny relativism's truth. As being as much a perspective as other claims, relativism's attempt to treat all other claims as perspectives would not be worth taking seriously because of the hypocrisy of its aforementioned paradox.

However, one would be mistaking the purpose of relativism completely by believing it false, simply because its central claim is unexempt from being a perspective. As a claim describing *all* views about the meaning of life as perspectives, including itself, its goal is to examine our anthropocentric claims about the

9. See Phillips, *Challenge of Relativism*.

philosophical problem from beyond human perception while attempting to remain intelligible; this impersonal view is impossible to communicate to humans without itself being expressed in a language familiar to us, and this is why it has the *appearance* of being logically inconsistent. But the "flaw" in one person, the relativist, attempting to examine all other persons' perspectives by making a claim beyond the limitations of his own perspective is that he must contradict himself to succeed.

From an anthropocentric standpoint, the supposed response by Taylor would be justified in exposing the hypocrisy of a relativist who uses his own perspective to express relativism about other people's so-called "perspectives." However, if I may borrow Taylor's phrase, "from without" the relativist's perspective, the world, unblemished by anthropogenic languages and propositional statements describing it, is truly indifferent to how we, mere, egocentric humans, perceive it; this includes the meaning of life that philosophers sometimes insist has "objective" answers or meaning, even while it is completely impossible for any one of us to perceive the desired objectivity beyond the veil of our own perceptions.

In other words, we cannot see beyond what we see and think beyond what we think to perceive any aspect of life "in and of itself," including its ultimate meaning—assuming it has one—and the same applies to all our sense perceptions. Neither could we ever determine whether—in principle—the meaning of life is objective or not; insisting otherwise only begs the question: how could we be sure of life's objective meaning without any justificatory basis other than having a "hunch"? The only things with which we are acquainted are our mind-dependent perspectives of the meaning of life, and if we adopt the linguistic method, we at least have an intersubjective means to do so. Our human inability to see beyond perspectives and discover the ultimate meaning of life is similar to what David Hume famously wrote about the nature of reality being forever beyond our comprehension:

> It is confessed, that the utmost effort of human reason
> is to reduce the principles, productive of natural phe-
> nomena, to a greater simplicity, and to resolve the many

> particular effects into a few general causes, by means of
> reasonings from analogy, experience, and observation.
> But as to the causes of these general causes, we should in
> vain attempt their discovery; nor shall we ever be able to
> satisfy ourselves, by any particular explication of them.
> These ultimate springs and principles are totally shut up
> from human curiosity and enquiry.[10]

So, even as relativism is theoretically false on paper and by human conventions of reasoning, its central claim is *ultimately* "true" from beyond our perspectives; the view beyond our perspectives is *indifferent* to whatever perceived weight we ascribe to our beliefs, and relativism attempts best to make this impersonal view intelligible.[11] But in being put into human words and through a relativist's own human perspective, relativism self-contradicts by rendering itself accessible to those who dare not attempt imagining what lies beyond the veil of perception.

As a consequence of relativism being *effectively* true from an impersonal view, albeit false on paper, there is nothing to prevent a relativist from treating Taylor's view as a perspective, save a non-subjective truth; the relativist is justified in treating the claim, "the point of a human being living is simply to be living," as a perspective, since Taylor had not provided any uncontrived reason for believing otherwise.

To unite all conflicting perspectives and dispose of relativism, we need an absolute, uncontrived standard that cannot be reduced to a mere "perspective." An uncontrived standard would prevent a relativist from privileging all perspectives, as equally true of their corresponding subject, by providing itself as a measurement for what is true and untrue.

For a standard to be uncontrived, it must be fact-based or, preferably, indubitable thanks to analytic truths, and these truths must be relevant to the life-problem in question, as well

---

10. *An Enquiry*, 29.

11. I use scare quotes around 'true' to allow for the position that truth is manmade, and if this is the case, then any suggestion that there is objective truth is mistaken; this may serve usefully in the final chapter of this book, when I turn to confront nihilism.

as demonstrable. Thankfully, this standard already exists in the English language we use, but disregarding English linguistics only reintroduces the problem of relativism *cum* skepticism and, by extension, nihilism. Other languages have their own standard(s) for how life-problems are intra-linguistically interpreted, but for this book, as stated from the beginning, I shall only solve the meaning of life in English through English linguistics.[12]

Before exploring this "uncontrived standard" in chapter 5, I shall illustrate perspectival relativism through a rude thought experiment that reifies its damaging implications to theories of life and demonstrate the *only* way to avert it. As we shall see in the following two sections, non-subjective theories of life are as susceptible as subjectivism to the threat of relativism and, by extension, nihilism and, to some extent, skepticism.

II

JONES AND SMITH

Suppose Jones asks Smith "what is the meaning of life?" and Smith replies with "red."

"I beg your pardon?" cries Jones, "What the heck is "red" supposed to *mean*? And how could life possibly mean 'red'?"

Smith proceeds to provide personal and awe-inspiringly sentimental anecdotes of how life came to mean redly to him and, being well-educated, proceeds to explain his belief through well-reasoned, eloquent arguments. But Jones, now irritated, retorts to Smith that life is "blue," citing exactly the same anecdotes and well-reasoned arguments Smith gave, except every reference of "red" is now replaced with "blue."

---

12. Languages such as Arabic and Russian lack the definite article 'the' wherever 'the meaning of life' is concerned and, thus, do not uniformly express it with precisely the same denotations as their English-language counterpart. This means that the answer to the meaning of life may not be the same through crosslinguistic examination. This shall become clear in chapter 6 after I unpack 'the meaning of life' word by word.

"This is preposterous!" responds Smith, who suspects Jones of being insincere, "Life cannot possibly mean bluely! It is red, I tell you! Red!"

In this bizarre debate, there is no winner between Jones and Smith, but neither is there a loser; both of them advance a color preference and propose either "red" or "blue" as being *the* answer to *the* meaning of life, and both answers are completely absurd. But could we truly dismiss their beliefs as false? The reader must remember—as I made implicit on numerous occasions—that relativism occurs whenever philosophers choose to disregard the rules of language, and, so, the short answer is "no." Views that should have been false from the outset are now truth-indeterminate perspectives, and as long as they do not self-contradict, each one is privileged as subjectively "true" about the meaning of life. Although I almost sympathize with those who reject the answers of Jones and Smith, "common sense" alone—whatever that means—cannot provide a sufficient basis for "refuting" a view on the meaning of life. After all, in the absence of pertinent facts and relevant analytic truths, one person's common sense is another's nonsense; without facts, everyone is an "expert" on life's meaning, and without kindred certainty to arithmetic, even if relativism is refuted, every non-analytic answer, including facts, is dubitable and therefore vulnerable to skepticism.

Suppose, now, Brown, a professor who taught a course on the meaning of life for fifty years, eavesdropped on the strange, never-ending debate between Jones and Smith and decides to intervene. Whatever professor Brown's reaction, whether he rebuts the answers of Jones and Smith with his own, questions their sincerity, or explains how both gentlemen's answers contradict his "common sense," the professor—no matter how accomplished and intellectually capable he is—*cannot* refute their colorful life-theories. If Brown were to truly defeat Jones and Smith, then he would need to make use of pertinent facts *with* relevant analytic truths that are demonstrably true and independent of a person's perspective. The exchanges between Jones and Smith may go on forever unless Brown makes the obvious, yet brilliant, suggestion of consulting an official, well-respected English dictionary and explains to Jones and Smith how English works.

So, what does a dictionary serve in this context? It limits the discussion of 'life' to how it is defined according to sociolinguistic conventions as old as civilization itself and beyond. These conventions, which include 'lexicography' and 'grammar,' among others, are implicitly agreed upon by anyone anytime they wish to understand and be understood by others. For we cannot stipulate new meanings or usages for preexisting words and expect that the vast sociolinguistic community will simply adopt such hasty and arbitrary changes. Too many sudden and drastic changes to language would undermine its learnability, practicability, and therefore its usefulness. The reasoning behind following these rules uniformly is pragmatic: if two people want to understand each other, they have to use words they mutually understand. If language is changing too quickly, then many more unnecessary dialects will result from those unable or unwilling to keep pace with a rapidly evolving language and, therefore, fewer people will understand each other. As being a reference for English sociolinguistic communities, a well-respected English dictionary would bar "red" and "blue" from being meaningful and relevant to 'life' because these arbitrary uses are outright violations of semantics. Any reasonable person, in most instances, is intellectually compelled to defer to how their society, and especially its expert linguists, agrees each word should be used. Of course, the exception is when a word has conflicting origins and the person raising questions of its conventional meaning provides credible, etymological evidence to support his proposal. However, the exception thereof does not apply to the meaning of life. For instance, each word that is found in 'the meaning of life' is unmysterious, and there is no room for disputing what is so easily known and accessible to even the dullest minds; they are frequently used terms, which are staples in the vocabularies of virtually every English-speaking adult, and challenging their conventional meanings would damage their intelligibilities. Therefore, Jones and Smith would be extremely unreasonable by persisting in their beliefs after listening to Brown's recommendation and having learned how the English language works.

Reasonableness aside, if we could learn from previous experiences, Brown's commendable suggestion would likely be met with shrugs, provided he is lucky enough to have relatively polite listeners; I find it rather optimistic to believe the mention of a dictionary will see an end to the insistence that life means redly for Smith or bluely for Jones. And despite similar absurdities between their beliefs and the beliefs of Jones and Smith, philosophers are, likewise, unlikely to change their minds; there are even those who devoted vast periods of their careers to solving the meaning of life, without paying sufficient attention to the fine-grained differences between how they and their peers "define" it.

If the Jones-and-Smith thought experiment seems too simplistic, inconceivable, and absurd to be realistic, then one needs to look no further than the contemporary philosophy-of-life discourses I had spent considerable time criticizing. For inasmuch as philosophers and thinkers writing on the philosophy of life may implicitly characterize themselves as "experts," their efforts over the course of decades culminated to nothing revelatory since the aforementioned subdiscipline's outset; we are nowhere closer to an actual answer in the philosophy of life since the day Confucius and his disciples grasped their reed pens and contemplated answering similar life-problems, e.g., "How should we live?"

III

A REAL-LIFE ANALOGUE TO THE DEBATE BETWEEN JONES AND SMITH

As a precursor to what comes next, Ayer presciently observed, "[T]here is no single thing of which it can truly be said that this is the meaning of life. All that can be said is that life has at various times a different meaning for different people, according as they pursue their several ends."[13] Although Ayer is mistaken in believing

13. "The Claims of Philosophy," 201.

nothing true could be said about the meaning of life, he is right about how divided people were then as they are now. Let us begin, then, with a handful of diverse examples by theorists of varying merit talking past each other. What should become evident is, yet, another stalemate, which I shall counter in the following chapter with a brief synopsis of how the English language philosophers typically abuse really works.

Professor Susan Wolf, who had taught and written on the meaning of life for two decades, described in her Tanner lectures a life "meaningful insofar as its subjective attractions are to things or goals that are objectively worthwhile."[14] Emeritus Professor Kekes' colleague from Columbia University, Professor Steven M. Cahn disagrees with Wolf. He asks, "[D]oes it make judging a person's life as meaningful or meaningless make sense? Susan Wolf thinks so. I do not."[15] Professor William Lane Craig disagrees with anyone who does not share his Christian view of the meaning of life. He writes, "If God does not exist, then life is futile. If God exists, then life is meaningful."[16] Deceased Professor Robert Nozick wrote, "Being the creator of all we see is not sufficient to endow his purposes with meaningfulness."[17] While I cannot think of any noteworthy philosopher of life who seriously subscribes to relativism, their aimless disagreements, which are inimical to any meaningful progress with the life-problem, prove *de facto* the contrary.

These superficially convincing "answers," whose plausibilities depends on each person's bias, often make quite the theatrical display until they are properly scrutinized. For example, could we determine which among the contemporary claims in the philosophy of life is right and which ones are wrong? No, not unless philosophers of life are able to non-subjectively demonstrate the truth-values of their claims. But none of the views, either in part or whole, are genuinely non-subjective. For a start, Wolf would need to elaborate properly on whether we could truly judge a project

14. "Meaning in Life" 96.
15. Cahn, "Meaningless Lives?", 89.
16. Craig, "Absurdity of Life," 56.
17. *Philosophical Explanations*, 590.

or activity as being "objectively worthwhile" without presupposing relativism.[18] To avoid skepticism, Craig must decisively explain how he came to be certain his Christian God gives life meaning in the place of some other god, e.g., Cthulhu. In every case, theorists inquiring about the meaning of life still have to answer its question properly, and this requires a demonstrably uncontrived standard. For, in the absence of relevant empirical facts or analytic truths, the theories Wolf and Craig present are as mind-bogglingly arbitrary perspectives as the answers of Jones and Smith. To use W. D. Rawls' famous example for this context, Wolf cannot establish as fact that there are any activities more worthwhile than counting blades of grass on park squares or well-trimmed lawns.[19] Neither is there an uncontrived authority for determining the truth of one religion's view of the meaning of life over one belonging to another. It is, after all, not uncommon for a theist to proclaim the views of his religion self-evidently true while maintaining all others mistaken. And if we supposed, as I did previously, Craig's God exists, it would not prevent a secular philosopher such as Nozick from replying, "Why not a God who created that God, and so forth?"[20] Although Nozick's response is potentially fallacious, since God Almighty is absolutely perfect and cannot have a cause other than

18. Wolf acknowledges by stating, "I must confess that I have no positive account of nonsubjective [*sic*.] value with which I am satisfied" ("Meaning in Life," 104); her softened position in her 2007 lectures contrasts her more forceful approach a decade earlier (see Wolf "Happiness and Meaning").

For each time Wolf proposes something, a counterexample can easily be constructed; for instance, "mindless, futile, never-ending tasks are likely meaningless," which Cahn quoted from Wolf, prompted him to respond that "physical conditioning is mindless, trying to persuade all others of your solutions to philosophical problems is futile, and seeking to eliminate diseases is never-ending" ("Meaningless Lives?", 90). Wolf essentially has no answer, for she is both insisting on certain "objectively worthwhile" activities and achievements while insisting that "my answers to all these questions are tentative" ("Meaning in Life" 96); she is therefore evading the burden of proof her position requires her to justify.

19. *Theory of Justice*, 379.

20. *Philosophical Explanations*, 591.

himself, one must note the differing theological interpretations of capabilities that are truly attributable to this "God."

If philosophers continue to overlook linguistics, who is to say Jones is *wrong* for preferring the color blue as the answer to the meaning of life over Wolf's or Craig's theory of life? Who is to say my religion truly solves the meaning of life and yours does not? Who is to say my preference for activities, as opposed to yours, is more meaningful for each person's life? No matter which theory is advanced, if it does not introduce a relevant field of expertise, then it is no different and no less bizarre than the disagreement between Jones and Smith. Whether the theories advanced are as complex as evaluating the meaning of every single event in a life or as awe-inspiringly simple as Smith's preference for red hues, they are absurd all the same.

Without linguistics, relativism is inevitable. If relativism is the case and perspectives take priority over the literal meaning of words, one may as well answer "is the cat on the mat?" instead of "what is the meaning of life?" After all, if perspectives determine the meaning of words rather than their *usages*, then there is nothing left to prevent the meaning of life from being literally indistinguishable from any other question imaginable. If the meaning of life is literally indistinguishable from other phrases and questions, then it becomes futile to answer it at all, since it may as well mean everything or nothing; one may as well "answer" the meaning of life with unintelligible roars and cacophonies, and it would be just as meaningful an answer as another.

IV

CONCLUSION

The inevitable outcome of the disagreement between Jones and Smith, as well as contemporary philosophy-of-life discussions without facts and analytic truths, is similar to the relativism Ayer foresaw, but worse; Jones lives in his "reality" and so does Smith and so do all the professors who espouse views unsupported by relevant facts and analytic truths, and the same is true for the rest of us.[21] In the absence of an unarbitrary and absolute standard, everyone becomes an all-knowing god with unfettered powers to redefine the meaning of life. And even if we suppose "common sense," "plausibility," or "intuitiveness" as a safeguarding substitute of a question's meaning in the place of facts and analytic truths, different persons have different interpretations of these safeguards as well. In the absence of science, there cannot be progress, and without it, one cannot be faulted for echoing Stephen Hawking's and Leonard Mlodinow's proclamation that "philosophy is dead."[22] The only way out of the compounded threat of skepticism, perspectival relativism, and nihilism is by treating the meaning of life as a problem of language and thus a scientifically solvable problem.

So, if we were to finally assume that language is the relevant field of expertise for solving the meaning of life, how does linguistics refute these quagmires of conceptually confused opinions? For the sake of philosophers who are relentlessly hostile toward my solution, I shall eventually start with extraordinarily uncontroversial premises whose rejection would be extraordinarily unreasonable by any theorist worthy of their professional prefix. This begins by understanding the self-evident purpose of the English language and establishing the less uncontroversial but generally accepted claim that linguistics is a science. As a science, linguistics would incentivize adherence to the literal and grammatical details of 'the meaning of life' by replacing conceptually confusing opinions with facts. And since linguistics includes the study of semantics or semasiology, among other conventions of English, it includes the use of analytic truths to solve the meaning of life. However, the following chapter shall not immediately introduce language, since there remain its critics, those I dub "anti-linguists," whose objections, however misguided, must be addressed beforehand.

Should my solution be rejected anyway, I invite theorists to justify the sorry relativistic setting of stalemated inquiries in the

---

21. This is, of course, with the exception of the man who solved the meaning of life.

22. *The Grand Design*, 5.

philosophy of life; presumably, the fundamentally justified answer is preferable to none at all. From this point onward, the growing list of consequences or philosopher-made problems, resulting from ignoring linguistics, shall include a scenario much harder to ignore than the one presented in this chapter. By then, it is doubtful that those who persist in rejecting linguistics are sincere in their criticisms, given that the alternative is far too impracticable to be worthy of being taken seriously.

Chapter 5

The Tower of Babel

With every contemporary theory of life proven to be either technically false or nonsensical, the steps that remain are naming and defining the life-problem and then solving it with the unquestionable truth I promised. Or so it seemed. Before I proceed with the meaning of life, what is to prevent my harshest adversaries from rejecting the answer I later provide, if only for the sake of doing so? As I had stated in this book's introductory chapter, an answer that is less than certain is effectively as useless as silence; skepticism only requires a proposition to have a single possibility of being false. Thus, an answer lacking definitiveness in the philosophy of life is not really an answer, much less an intellectually satisfying one. But even while my answer in chapter 6 is analytically derived from what the life-problem denotes and is, thus, *apodictically* true in the way 'a 'bachelor' is an unmarried man' is indubitable, is it enough? Could philosophers *still* choose to disregard the language in which 'the meaning of life' formally appears? For example, suppose Baggini were attentive to the conventions of formal English; could he be justified in positing multiple kinds of meanings, even as "meaning" in 'the meaning of life' is singular? Are Kai Nielsen, R. W. Hepburn, and Joshua Seachris justified in rejecting the semantics of 'the meaning of life' that partially figures into the theory I later provide? A third step that preempts the absurd responses of *anti-linguists* is therefore needed.

To ensure my adversaries know the outcome of rejecting my answer is not inconsequential but carries with it *great catastrophes*, I shall, for the most part, explain *how the English language really works*. If philosophers truly understood the ultimate purpose of the English language, they would also understand that disregarding its conventions is as irrational as it is destructive and in no way advances their theoretical ambitions. For it is almost as Adams, and Cottingham had predicted, but not quite: linguistics demonstrates that there are *indeed* category-mistakes and signs of conceptual confusions. However, neither stem from 'the meaning of life' itself; rather, if they understood linguistics, they would likewise understand these issues, which include the philosopher-made problems of perennial problems, truth-indeterminacies, and fallacies we encountered in chapters 2–4, resulted from technically false or nonsensical claims. As we saw again and again, disregarding linguistics only manages to stagnate the philosophy of life and propagate needless, nonsensical speculation; the alternative, which I present, requires no such need for conjectures and carries with it relevant facts and analytic truths that decisively halt relativism and skepticism. However, nihilism is an issue I leave for the concluding chapter until we have a better picture of 'meaning.'

Aside from the explanation of formal English's inner workings herein, we shall finally learn the truth of this "meaning," which philosophers unsparingly used with carelessness, near the end of chapter 6. By the end of this chapter, philosophers shall run out of all sensible excuses imaginable for refusing the linguistic method for solving the meaning of life.

I

ANTI-LINGUISTS

Since the earliest verbatim mentions of 'the meaning of life' appeared in literature, the thought of language as the key to solving it eluded virtually every thinker, including those who were aware of linguistics.

Early thinkers in the philosophy of life, such as Arthur Schopenhauer, and Leo Tolstoy, never once considered the fundamental importance of the words and their arrangements that appeared before their very eyes. The closest the latter came to acknowledging linguistics was his abrupt dismissal of all branches of science, much like Cottingham's adamant rejection of "rational scientific culture" two centuries later (as shown in chapter 2). Tolstoy wrote, "[T]he fields of knowledge not only failed to lead me out of my despair but rather increased it."[1] Elsewhere, he clarified that "[r]ational knowledge led me to the conclusion that life is meaningless,"[2] which is strikingly similar to the pessimistic attitudes of Adams, and Cottingham toward the study of language.

It was not until the latter half of the twentieth century that academic interest in the language underlying 'the meaning of life' went from being virtually nonexistent to *barely* noticeable. But this "linguistic" interest—if it could actually be called such—was very short-lived, half-hearted, and had nothing to do with the formal study of the language underlying the original life-problem; rather, the philosophers who briefly discussed linguistics implicitly or explicitly did so for the sole purpose of dismissing it, either in whole or in part and without providing any actual arguments.

In 1964, Nielsen was the first philosopher of life to *explicitly* acknowledge linguistics and attempt its use to solve the meaning of life; he did so without explaining linguistics or making use of the conventions of formal English, such as discussing syntax, morphology, or referencing the strict, literal meaning of words. Still, Nielsen could barely contain his enthusiasm as he wrote in his first page, "American and English academic philosophy has in various degrees 'gone linguistic.' "[34] However, his overly optimistic tone quickly changed. By the second page of his twenty-three-page paper, ironically named "Linguistic Philosophy and 'the Meaning

---

1. *Confession*, 48.

2. Tolstoy, *Confession*, 60.

3. "Linguistic Philosophy," 233.

4. Although the Nielsen paper I am referencing was published later than 1964, its words are more or less the same as its original publication.

of Life,' " Nielsen devoted *one paragraph* to dismissing a subdiscipline of linguistics, namely, its branch concerning semantics or semasiology:

> the mark (token) "meaning" in "What is the meaning of Life?" has a very different use than it has in "What is the meaning of 'obscurantist'?" "What is the meaning of 'table'?" "What is the meaning of 'good'?" "What is the meaning of 'science'?" and "What is the meaning of 'meaning'?" In these other cases we are asking about the meaning or use of the word or words, and we are requesting either a definition of the word or an elucidation or description of the word's use. But in asking: "What is the meaning of Life?" we are not asking—or at least this is not our central perplexity—about "What is the meaning of the word 'Life'?" What [*sic.*] then [*sic.*] are we asking?[5]

Has the reader noticed anything especially peculiar about what was written? Nielsen is the sole author of his article and used what is known as a 'nosism' when he wrote "we" in "we are not asking ..." It is a well-known strategy employed by philosophers to bluff an appearance of implicit plausibility or to deflect attention from themselves whenever they are *alone* in advancing a claim lacking argumentative support. For instance, had Nielsen referred to himself with 'I' instead, he would have likely been expected to defend his claim or run the risk of appearing unconvincing and very arrogant. Apart from his cunning, Nielsen did not provide a single argument for why "we are not asking" "about the meaning or use of the word" 'life'; he only *insisted* that any literal reading of "what is the meaning of life?" is not the case.

A few years later, R. W. Hepburn, who was influenced by Nielsen's 1964 paper, began by deciding whether to inquire "what is the meaning of life?" linguistically or non-linguistically; this was expressed in the form of a dilemma: "either renounce the vocabulary—as too deeply entangled with unacceptable beliefs, or to radically redefine the terms 'meaning,' 'meaningful' and their

5. "Linguistic Philosophy," 234.

cognates."[6] He eventually opts to both renounce the vocabulary and radically redefine 'the meaning of life' through a theory now known as 'the amalgam thesis'; it is the theory wherein words and definitions are malleable to the supposed intention of the person who asks about the meaning of life, as we shall later see.

On the next page of his article, he slyly equivocated, "A life is not a statement, and cannot therefore have linguistic meaning."[7] But it is unclear what inspired his belief that linguistics entails the claim that 'life is a statement' or entails renouncing the vocabulary of 'the meaning of life' as lacking linguistic meaning. First, 'the meaning of life' having "linguistic meaning" is not tantamount to the imaginary linguist's claim that "life is a statement." As a phrase *per se*, the former has linguistic meaning because it comprises *literally* meaningful words that are linguistically *interpretable*. Whereas the reference of 'a life' does not have linguistic meaning because it overtly involves a living or formerly living creature, which obviously comprises or comprised cells instead of words. However, the words 'a' and 'life' *per se* cannot be denied as having linguistic meaning insofar as they are semantically meaningful words. Second, these claims are mutually independent since 'the meaning of life' has a different reference than the phrase 'a life'; the former is a phrase making a definite reference of an abstraction, i.e., "meaning" in 'the meaning of life,' and the latter makes an indefinite reference to some living or formerly living creature. So, one claim (i.e., "A life is not a statement") being false does not necessarily make the other false because there is no interdependency between the two. Hepburn is obviously right that 'a life' is not a *statement*; for even by the opinion of actual linguists, a sentence fragment cannot be a statement, unless we consider it as part of the paradoxical statement 'a life is not a statement,' which is itself a statement and one belonging to the *Liar's Paradox*, e.g., 'this statement is false.' But Hepburn is mistaken that the strawman he constructed from an implicit phrase (i.e., 'A life is a statement') is

6. Hepburn, "Questions," 125.
7. Hepburn, "Questions," 126.

an argument against the claim that the meaning of life is linguistically meaningful.

Although Hepburn admits, "At the start of this article I mentioned one terse and gruff dismissal [of the linguistic meaning],"[8] which I quoted in the previous paragraph, he carries through with it anyway; he concludes, "The vocabulary of meaning can thus be rejected *en bloc* . . . the language of the meaning of life is not indispensable."[9] Aside from his "terse and gruff dismissal," he, at least, provides what appears to be a reason for rejecting "linguistic meaning," but not quite:

> But [*sic.*] admittedly [*sic.*] we do use the word 'meaning' outside of linguistic contexts. We speak of the meaning of a gesture, of a transaction, [*sic.*] of a disposition of troops; and in such cases [*sic.*] we are speaking of the point or purpose or end of an act or set of acts. This usage suggests an equation between meaningfulness and purposiveness. For a life to be meaningful, it must be purposeful: or—to make life meaningful is to pursue valuable ends.[10]

By suggesting "an equation between meaningfulness and purposiveness," Hepburn is proposing that *we*—and not just him—are implying that "meaning" in 'the meaning of life' means "worthwhile quality; purpose,"[11] the very equivocation that Baggini committed, which I pointed out in chapter 2. For those unfamiliar with what Hepburn is suggesting, the amalgam thesis is the claim that we could substitute words in 'the meaning of life,' whose relevance depends on our purposeful intentions—whatever they are—of the person asking "what is the meaning of life?" However, Hepburn is conveniently silent about whether we also use 'meaning' within linguistic contexts, which implies the nuance denoting "what is meant by a word, text, concept, or action."[12] Whereas he eagerly

8. Hepburn, "Questions," 138.

9. Hepburn, "Questions," 140.

10. Hepburn, "Questions," 126.

11. *Concise Oxford Dictionary*, 10th ed. (1999), s.v. "meaning."

12. *Concise Oxford Dictionary*, 10th ed. (1999), s.v. "meaning."

states examples for what it is to "pursue valuable ends" "to make life meaningful," he does not bother to clarify what makes him so keenly adamant about rejecting the latter aforementioned definition of 'meaning' as being a reference of "meaning" in 'the meaning of life.'

So—once again—as we saw with Nielsen, Hepburn insisted on rejecting semantics, but the latter went further by dismissing linguistics entirely (by also renouncing vocabulary) without providing a single argument against it; that is, unless the equivocation and strawman fallacies he committed count as "reasonings" against the aptly put "linguistic meaning."

Although Nielsen's, and Hepburn's dismissals of linguistics occurred by the *second* page of their papers in few sentences, Seachris remarkably managed to dismiss it even sooner in fewer words. The latter wrote in the first page of his paper: "One option is to retain the word 'meaning' [in 'the meaning of life'] and secure a usage for it that applies to non-linguistic phenomena, [*sic.*] we are not asking for the *semantic* meaning of the word 'life.' "[13] For a third time, the patronizing nosism "we" resurfaces from yet another sole author of a philosophy paper. But he implicitly claims, anyway, to know on the behalf of his readers and colleagues what *we*—his readers—are *allowed* to mean and not mean when asking "what is the meaning of life?" After pensively listing his options, it is not long before he decides, "In this paper [*sic.*] *I* [but not *we*] take the road less traveled and adopt the first approach."[14]

Nielsen, Hepburn, and Seachris, and Adams, and Cottingham in chapter 2, represent the bulk, if not all, of the philosophers of life who acknowledged linguistics; yet none of them understood what they so hastily dismissed. Not a single among them refuted linguistics as a method of explanation to the meaning of life, much less explained what they were so audaciously certain about dismissing. But could anti-linguists simply insist that language has no importance in determining the meaning of life? After all, Hepburn insists "the language of the meaning of life is not indispensable."

13. Seachris, "Life as Narrative," 5.

14. Seachris, "Life as Narrative," 6; my emphasis.

Perhaps a tale of a Medieval king who shared a similar, anti-linguistic aspiration, could provide us useful analogical insight on ignoring linguistics.

II

PHILOSOPHUS NON EST SUPRA GRAMMATICAM

Legend has it that when the king reigning over Hungary, Croatia, Germany, and Bohemia went before the Council of Constance (in 1414 CE) to end the Hussites' rebellion, he misspoke 'schisma' by saying "schismam."[15] In the midst of his speech condemning Church reformer Jan Hus, Cardinal Placentius interrupted King Sigismund to inform him that 'schisma' is a neuter word and cannot be used with a feminine Latin suffix. But instead of simply acknowledging his grammatical error and moving on with his deliverance, the king, who is self-evidently not a grammarian, interrogated Placentius about how the cardinal came to be sure 'schisma' is correct. So, the latter replied that Alexander Gallus, an old schoolmaster, being a monk and grammarian like himself, told him so, and the exchange went on for a little while longer.

As grammarians, Cardinal Placentius and schoolmaster Alexander Gallus are in a position of authority to tell others (but not proclaim) how and how not to use Latin words, even to a soon-to-be-Holy-Emperor-of-Rome; they are, after all, *qualified* experts in Latin. However, King Sigismund decided—anyway—that he will decree his mistaken use "schismam" a new usage for 'schisma,' just because he can; he declared, "Ego sum Rex Romanus et super grammaticam" ("I am King of the Romans and above grammar") and Placentius famously retorted, "Caesar non est supra grammaticos," or, roughly, "Caesar is not above grammarians."[16]

According to the myth, King Sigismund either never succeeded in changing the usage of 'schisma' or never followed

15. See Kind, *Über die Bildung*; Carlyle, *History of Friedrich II*; and Müeller, *The Science of Language*.

16. Carlyle, *History of Friedrich II*, 134.

through. But even if he did, he would have done so at the expense of every other Latin speaker; it would unnecessarily inconvenience all those who, unlike King Sigismund, unassumingly followed the language's rules and humbly learned from their misuses of words whenever they were made aware. So, why should King Sigismund *not* be above grammar? Let us briefly consider some likely implications if King Sigismund were to have his way with Latin grammar; from this scenario, we see what could have resulted from the boundless pride that overcame the king and, to this day, intoxicates philosophers to audaciously dismiss a language's rules whenever they do not suit them.

Suppose King Sigismund made his decree and "schismam" became a Latin word that all Latin speakers must suddenly use. What is to prevent other high-ranking members from various occupations, be it the clergy, military, government, business, professoriate, or royal families, from likewise rewriting a language? Assuming there are thousands of high-ranking persons who similarly swell with pride, it is quite possible that most of them would be tempted to be above grammar instead of properly learning it; an authoritarian individual like King Sigismund sets a very encouraging self-exculpating "precedent," as lawyers and judges call it, for those struggling with similar temptations. This could mean thousands of new, idiosyncratic terms muddying the increasingly polluted waters of languages, as well as a departure from etymologists, philologists, and phonologists determining a word's form according to preestablished, linguistic patterns. For instance, between the thirteenth and seventeenth centuries, something of this sort occurred with the English language prior to its standardization; the *Great Vowel Shift* of that period was due in large part to forthcoming generations of English speakers ignoring the Middle English pronunciations of every long vowel and some consonants, especially what are now called *silent letters*.[1718]

17. See Stockwell, "A Millennial Perspective."

18. The Great Vowel Shift owes its name to Otto Jespersen (1860–1943), a specialist of the English language grammar.

Once a violation of formal English is tolerated in academic settings, such as the philosophy of life, this tolerated error invites further violations of conventions until the language thereof becomes increasingly unrecognizable. Over the course of a few years, the changes are unnoticeable, but with enough time, the language will become as radically different from itself as it did for the English language between its middle period and the present.

I shall briefly explain the inner workings of the English language in the next section and then draw upon the consequences of its misuse in section VI.

III

HOW THE ENGLISH LANGUAGE REALLY WORKS

The overarching purpose of the English language, as being a *shared* language, is interpersonally intelligible communication.[19] (For if this were not the case, I cannot imagine there being any other purpose befitting the way English is *primarily* used.) Intelligible dialogues between a vast number of English speakers require language conventions to be commonly and consistently practiced among people, with points of reference for word usage, e.g., well-respected dictionaries and grammar books, being easily accessible. As it is embedded in words and part of a language self-evidently intended to be interpersonally intelligible, 'the meaning of life' is no exception to rules governing formal English.

English is intelligible between people because its symbols, i.e., alphabetic letters, words, phrases, and sentences, *consistently* reflect conventional semantics, phonology, prosody, morphology,

---

19. I use the word "interpersonally" to differentiate between a person communicating with himself from two or more individuals communicating between each other. For example, a student taking notes during a lecture is, in effect, communicating with himself at a later time, when he must review what he had written. If I had not made this distinction, then one could mistake me as allowing for the possibility of interpreting the meaning of life through idiolects; strictly speaking, idiolects are intelligible insofar as they are still understood by oneself.

and syntax; the latter two are usually considered as 'grammar.'[20] Whereas a person's inconsistent use or misuse of the English language will confuse other English-speaking persons. Even sarcasm, which often belies semantics, must implicitly contrast something intelligible for it to produce potentially humorous or denigrating effects, and this requires juxtaposed consistency with the context-sensitive semantics it is usually intended to contradict.

The other reason English is intelligible is that its aforementioned convention rules have some permanency. Notwithstanding slang and academic jargon, formal English stays relatively the same over the course of extended periods of time so it does not have to be learned multiple times over the course of a person's life. For instance, Charles Dickens' books, which are over 100 years old, are fairly easy to read to this day, and they are among the most-read books in literature. Also, the words added or removed from an English dictionary each quarter-year usually numbers in the hundreds, versus the 171,476 words, excluding subentries, of the second edition, twenty-volume Oxford English Dictionary in current use. Over the course of a lifetime, only a fraction of the entire English lexis changes. Even English-speaking countries, separated by borders and oceans, have not recently experienced a significant dialectical divergence between themselves in several centuries; it is fairly common for speakers from Ireland, Scotland, Wales, England, the United States, Canada, Australia, and New Zealand to understand each other, especially in formal English. Likewise, we must inquire about the meaning of life within formal English rules if we should have any hope in keeping its discourse intelligible.

The official sources of reference for the usage of the English language are well-respected dictionaries such as the *Oxford English Dictionary* and *Merriam-Webster*, and style manuals *Oxford Style Guide* and *Chicago Manual of Style*. And these official records are in place to keep the English language consistent so that it stays interpersonally intelligible, as opposed to gradually becoming idiolectic. If inquiries concerning the meaning of life are not done with these official references in mind, we risk kindred scenarios

20. See *Concise Oxford Dictionary*, 10th ed. (1999), s.v. "grammar."

to the Jones-and-Smith debate. For it should go without mention that philosophers using certain key terms, especially 'the,' 'meaning,' and 'life,' must make clear which homonyms they intend and respect their usages. Otherwise, philosophers would be talking past each other by using various nuances of the same words as we saw in the previous chapter and especially with Baggini, and Cottingham in chapter 2.

Now that the purpose of language is clear, and we know some reasons for respecting its conventions, could it be said that the study of the English language is a science? Yes, according to *The Concise Oxford Dictionary*, 'science' is "the intellectual and practical activity encompassing the systematic study of the structure and behaviour of the physical and natural world through observation and experiment."[21] Linguistics is defined as "the scientific study of language and its structure."[22] Oxford, which is generally considered the foremost authority on the English language and whose university was founded as early as *c.* 1096 CE, states that each of their dictionaries requires over 250 specialists. These specialists, which include lexicographers, etymologists, philologists, grammarians, phonologists, among others, research, analyze, and document the English language's changes and developments; these changes and developments require specialists to leave their offices, go outside in the world, and observe how ordinary English speakers and writers in English sociolinguistic communities use words. Thus, linguistics is not always an armchair profession. But as I argued the need to distinguish between abstract and physical sciences in chapters 2 and 3, one should not mistake 'science' as precluding some of the purely analytic work of linguists.

So, based on how 'science' and 'linguistics' are defined and the above reasoning, it would be, by the above definitions, literally impossible and factually false to deny that linguistics is real science and the English language is not its field of expertise. This also makes official, English-language references, such as the utmost-respected Oxford dictionaries, authorities on lexis, morphology, phonology,

21. *Concise Oxford Dictionary*, 10th ed. (1999), s.v. "science."
22. *Concise Oxford Dictionary*, 10th ed. (1999), s.v. "linguistics."

and semantics, and Oxford grammar books, authorities on syntax and morphology or grammar. Browsing a dictionary or a grammar book is effectively the same as consulting a few hundred scientists for their qualified opinions on a subject, instead of the blind speculations of philosophers well beyond their credentials. Most importantly, the status of linguistics as a 'science' means there are language-based *facts* that apply to the meaning of life, as a phrase embedded in English. Furthermore, the proposition 'a 'bachelor' is an unmarried man' represents only one of many language-based analytic truths; every statement involving a formal definition in a well-respected dictionary is an analytic truth, including the meaning of the words forming 'the meaning of life,' and they are as certain as '2 + 2 = 4.'

Apart from the lexis and its semantics, there are conventional rules that are likewise analytic truths, some of which I mentioned in the introduction of this book. For instance, ' "meaning" in 'the meaning of life' is singular' is an analytic truth based in grammar; it is *without exception* singular since its denial is a contradiction and always false. As we shall see in the following section, violations of semantic and grammatical rules ultimately bring about devastating consequences above and beyond impossibilities on paper, which inconveniences *everyone* and not just philosophers of life.

When developments and changes in the English language are documented, they are formalized into official words that are added to a dictionary each quarter-year. Dictionaries and other English points of reference are the safeguards that keep morphology, semantics, compound semantics (e.g., the literal meanings of idioms), syntax, and pronunciations as consistent as possible. Without them, English would change more frequently over relatively shorter periods of time. For instance, Thomas Hobbes' 372-year-old *Leviathan* or Shakespeare's 417-year-old *Macbeth* remain readable to this very day. Whereas Geoffrey Chaucer's *The Canterbury Tales* (1387 CE) of the Middle English period (c. 1150–1500 CE) is strenuously half-readable, and the epic *Beowulf* (c. 1000 CE) of the Old English period (c. 450–1150 CE) is completely alien to the modern English reader.[23] The latter two books were written prior to what is, perhaps arguably, regarded as the first English dictionary, published in 1604; in any case—and according to a former chief editor of the Oxford English Dictionary—the proliferation of monolingual English dictionaries did not occur until the seventeenth century.[24] Here are some excerpts from *Beowulf, The Canterbury Tales, Romeo and Juliet,* and *Leviathan,* respectively:

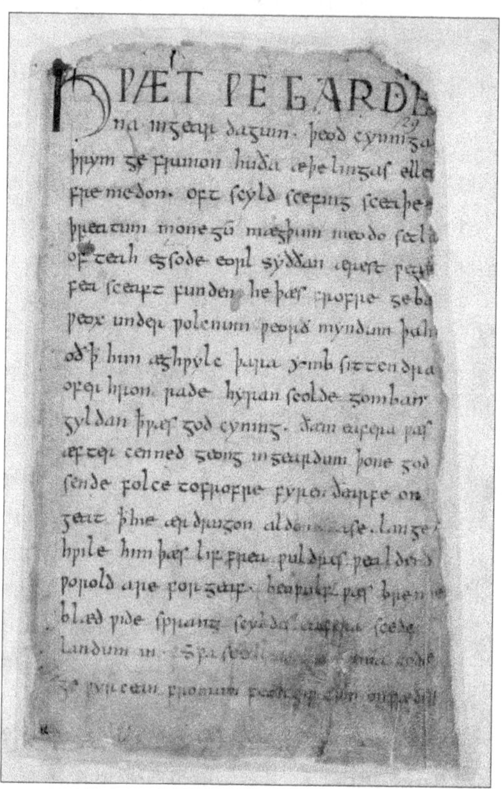

Figure 1. The first page of the first folio of the *Beowulf* manuscript. Cotton MS Vitellius A.XV, f. 132 (The . . . Unknown artist tenth-eleventh century). British Library, London, UK, British Library Board. Copyright to the British Library Board. All Rights Reserved. Bridgeman Images.

23. For more information about Old and Middle English, see Durkin, "Old English," and "Middle English," respectively.

24. See bibliography note on Simpson, "First Dictionaries."

HPÆT ÞE GARDE na ınzear dagum · þeod cynınga
þrym gefrunon huða æþelıngaſ ellen fremedon .[25]

Whilom, as olde stories tellen us
There was a duc that highte theseus
Of atthenes he was lord and governour
And in his tyme swich a conquerour
That gretter was ther noon under the sonne[26]

Figure 2. The first page of "The Knight's Tale" in the Ellesmere manuscript of the *Canterbury Tales*. The Ellesmere Chaucer mssEL 26 C 9. Courtesy of The Huntington Library, San Marino, California. Rights to the image reproduction are held by the respective copyright holder.

25. Quoted in Gelderen, *Analyzing Syntax*, 33; see also figure 1.

26. Compare figure 2 with Chaucer, "The Knight's Tale," verses 859–63.

> Life's but a walking Shadow, a poore Player,
> That ſtruts and frets his howre vpon the Stage,
> And then is heard no more. It is a Tale
> Told by an Ideot, full of sound and fury,
> Signifying nothing.[27]

> Whatever therefore is consequent to a time of Warre, where every man is Enemy to every man ; the same is consequent to the time, wherein men live without other security, than what their own strength, and their own invention shall furnish them withall. In such condition, there is no place for Industry ; because the fruit thereof is uncertain : and consequently no Culture of the Earth ; no Navigation, nor use of the commodities that may be imported by Sea ; no commodious Building ; no Instruments of moving, and removing such things as require much force ; no Knowledge of the face of the Earth ; no account of Time ; no Arts ; no Letters ; no Society ; and which is worst of all, continual feare, and danger of violent death ; And the life of a man, solitary, poore, nasty, brutish, and short.[28]

Beowulf was written near the end of the Old English period and *Canterbury Tales* a few centuries after the Middle English period began; both of them were written at least several centuries before the first monolingual English dictionary (1604) and came either before or during the Great Vowel Shift (between the thirteenth and seventeenth centuries). In the approximately 400 years between these first two excerpts (*c.* 1000–1387 CE), the English between them had evolved so far apart that neither are remotely similar. Even the letters used are different from each other, as the futhorc and alphabetical systems are different. Moreover, the first among the two excerpts is completely unintelligible, and the second is barely understandable to a modern English reader. Whereas the

27. Foreman, "Macbeth in Elizabethan Pronunciation," YouTube video, uploaded February 3, 2021, https://www.youtube.com/watch?v=cuavC5dXCi8, 00:01:58, compare with Shakespeare, *Macbeth*, lines 2345–2350, Act V, Scene V.

28. Hobbes, *Leviathan*, 96–7.

language appearing in the latter two excerpts (from *Macbeth* [1606] and *Leviathan* [1651]) are remarkably similar to modern English. The 400 years of English between 1600 and 2000 CE, as compared to the approximately 400 years between 1000 and 1387 CE, appears to have undergone a far less drastic language evolution, at least not enough change to make several-hundred-year-old writings unreadable to the modern-English reader. So, it must not be a coincidence that the increasing prominence of dictionaries in the seventeenth century stabilized the chaotically unwieldy evolution of the English language by standardizing lexical spelling, their corresponding word families, and pronunciation.

Robert Cawdrey's *Table Alphabeticall* (1604) was certainly not the first dictionary of any language, as many came centuries before it, but it was the first known monolingual *English* dictionary; it was also the first to organize its approximately 3,000 English words in alphabetical order. However, this is but one of several factors needed to consolidate the English language's tendency to evolve rapidly and chaotically. The second factor occurred centuries prior, in 1439 CE, when Johannes Gutenberg invented the printing press. Although the printing press had existed in various forms for many centuries before his time, Gutenberg's revolutionary invention was more user-friendly and allowed for the mass production of books, including dictionaries, and, thus, made the propagation of official English references possible and more accessible. The third factor is the inception of grammar school.

During the English Reformation in the sixteenth century, when King Henry VIII famously rejected papal supremacy and proclaimed himself the supreme head of the Church of England, he seized ownership of all English monasteries and ordered their dissolution. Before then, these religious monasteries partly served as education centers for the privileged few among English youth. But upon King Edward VI's reign (King Henry's son), the money seized from the treasuries of erstwhile monasteries helped fund the creation of grammar schools. And in turn, these schools, which, unlike their predecessors, specialized in teaching English and Latin language structures, increased literacy because they were accessible to more students (other than the privileged few).

Knowledge of languages' structures is what limited one of the driving forces of unchecked language evolution: human error, the arrogance of incorrigibility, and the distorting, dialectic effects of oral communication (e.g., the Great Vowel Shift). However, unchecked language evolution still remains a threat to standardized English while its participants refuse to follow its rules.

IV

THE GREAT CATASTROPHES

To fully appreciate the absurdity of what anti-linguists Nielsen, Hepburn, and Seachris propose, let us do as they say and witness the full force of their proposals' implications.

While bearing in mind that the ultimate purpose of the English language is interpersonally intelligible communication, what is the worst that could happen as a result of disregarding the semantics of the phrase 'the meaning of life'? Obviously, we would not understand it; the phrase 'the meaning of life' would strike us with a perplexity akin to a phrase in an unfamiliar language. For the sake of clarity, observe the following:

1. 生活,

2. प्रयोजन, and

3. ystyr.

Did the reader understand all the words represented in (1), (2), and (3)? (Browsing a multilingual dictionary is cheating, since it presupposes what the anti-linguists unanimously deny is the case for the meaning of life: semantics.) Without any literal meaning, 'the meaning of life' would be no more than an arrangement of alien symbols, similar to how one perceives some or all the above non-English words.

I doubt *this* is what the anti-linguists had in mind when they insisted on ignoring literal meaning, since the austere endeavor is self-evidently futile. In fairness, perhaps the anti-linguists did not really mean to disregard semantics, but instead preclude it as being the answer to 'the meaning of life' *per se*. But even then, we run into the same difficulty encountered in chapter 2: the fact "meaning" in 'the meaning of life' is singular technically disqualifies any claim with multiple meanings.

Since semantics represents an entire category of meaning, i.e., literal meaning, anti-linguists cannot propose *both* a non-literal meaning of 'life' while also *presupposing* its literal meaning. Otherwise, the theory of life proposing a single, non-literal meaning would still be technically disqualified for proposing multiple meanings, as it must presuppose literal meaning as well. So, theories proposing a non-literal meaning would actually be proposing at least two kinds of meanings anyway, a contradiction of the singular "meaning" in 'the meaning of life.' For the very act of *understanding* the phrase 'the meaning of life' or writing about it in words that readers can literally understand *presumes* its literal meaning. This also means that Seachris cannot possibly secure "a usage" of 'meaning' for "non-linguistic phenomena" of life or the meaning of life without writing about it in literally meaningful words.

Suppose, then, we, at last, try it Hepburn's way and renounce "linguistic meaning," since "a life is not a statement" and "the language of the meaning of life is not indispensable." By rejecting "linguistic meaning," Hepburn is not only renouncing vocabulary and semantics but also every formal English convention, including grammar and the words forming 'the meaning of life.' In doing so, Hepburn is able to avoid the technical disqualification involving singular meaning, as well as reword and "radically redefine" certain terms in the phrase 'the meaning of life' however he pleases. However, in allowing for the freedom to substitute 'the meaning of life' in whole or part, with words or phrases that *seem* "relevant" to it, we risk re-confronting the problems raised in chapter 4. What is to say one family of related life-problems or terms counts as substitutable with 'the meaning of life' in the place of another or a family of completely unrelated words or problems? Without a strict, unarbitrary meaning to words and phrases, Hepburn's stipulations of words that count as relevant or irrelevant to the meaning of life carry as much weight as the opinions of everyone else. No matter what answer Hepburn gives for 'the meaning of life,' the problem of skepticism *cum* relativism is inescapable and undefeatable. Once relativism is reintroduced through unsubstantiated claims, it would be impossible without formal English conventions for Hepburn to guard 'the meaning of life' against its substitution with phrases like 'the cat is on the mat'; any non-analytic or non-factual claim that does not self-contradict, including irrelevant analytic truths or facts, could be reduced to a mere perspective or opinion with no more significance than another. Thus, Hepburn's proposal, as with every other theory of life, fails to non-arbitrarily limit all imaginable answers that qualify and do not qualify for "what is the meaning of life?" Without formal English conventions, 'the meaning of life' could mean virtually everything or nothing, since the literal boundaries that distinguish words and phrases from others are no longer in play. In effect, even if he is radically free to renounce formal English, Hepburn's proposal still results in nonsense. But if he were to retain semantics and limit his proposal to solely rewording or rephrasing 'the meaning of life,' Hepburn would then be inquiring about a different life-problem, which would no longer be philosophically interesting. In any case, Hepburn dismisses the very conventions that are indispensable for his readers to literally understand his paper, which is as absurd as it is self-defeating.

There is no chance that the proposals severally advanced by Nielsen, Hepburn, and Seachris are remotely true because stripping 'the meaning of life' of its semantics prevents answers pertaining to it from being truth-evaluable. As I had written in chapter 3, truth-indeterminate claims are incapable of being impossible, unlikely, probable, or indubitable because they are nil-valued and inert. This means that, unlike Baggini, and Cottingham who had at the very least provided technically false answers, the proposals advanced by the anti-linguists cannot even be false because they are absurd and nonsensical. However, as I wrote from the beginning of this chapter, what is to prevent my harshest adversaries from rejecting the answer to the meaning of life I later provide, if only for the sake of doing so? And what are these "great catastrophes"?

Suppose Smith learns how the English language works and, upon browsing an Oxford dictionary for key words, joins anti-linguists in dismissing the language underlying 'the meaning of life' anyway. Why should Smith stop disregarding the English language after he reinvents 'the meaning of life'? What prevents Smith from disregarding and reinventing the entire English language and, further, every form of interpersonally intelligible communication, including sign and body language? There are hundreds of words in the subdisciplines of philosophy and thousands more disciplines other than philosophy that are speculative and, likewise, open to interpretation and nevertheless important to us, much like our desire to know the meaning of life. In ethics, for instance, terms such as 'justice,' 'good,' 'bad,' 'duty,' and 'obligation,' had eluded philosophers for centuries, and the same is true of 'consciousness,' 'quale,' among others, in the philosophy of mind. None of the aforementioned terms could be explained non-circularly, and there is no indication of progress or any foreseeable prospects of agreement in ethics at least. By the full extent of the anti-linguists' proposals, Smith cannot stop at 'the meaning of life' after substituting its words; he must similarly apply the same disregard to all words and phrases of some particular interest or another, similar to what philosophers have done with the philosophy of life. Further, upon realizing that every convention of English can be explained away as being "not indispensable" and being the consistent anti-linguist he is, Smith must likewise do away with every language, which, like English, is conventional, including common body-language expressions.

Although one may criticize this silly example as most improbable and find no connection between the rejection of 'the meaning of life' and reinventing every language, logical justification demands consistency! The anti-linguists cannot simply cherry-pick when and when not to disregard the English language while the consequences of doing so are too unpalatable. If the language of 'the meaning of life' is not indispensable, then, by that token, there is nothing that logically prevents the dismissal of every other word, phrase, and all convention-based, interpersonally intelligible languages. But what if the anti-linguists are unbothered by this pernicious scenario and continue on with their everyday lives as if "nothing" had happened?

After dismissing every language, Smith decides to carry on with his life as usual. When he visits a coffee shop, a barista cheerfully asks him, "How may I take your order, sir?" Smith has two options: either renounce his philosophy as being too impracticable or cherry-pick when and when not to disregard language at the expense of being a hypocrite. Let us assume Smith is sensible and briefly suspends his anti-linguistic inclination; he hypocritically orders his coffee in terms the barista understands by following commonly understood English conventions: "I would like a black coffee, please." What has just occurred? Smith decided to use mutually understood words according to their literal meaning, arrange them in their rightful sequence, and pronounce them properly. But something else happened as well: Smith is sane enough not to wholeheartedly ignore the language's conventions, even while logical consistency demands it, because everyday life without the proper use of language is socially impossible. Not only are the anti-linguists' proposals absurd on paper, but Smith had just proven they are also impracticable in the real world. Had Smith spoken his own idiolect to the barista, he would have eventually been asked to leave, after causing the barista much confusion.

Suppose now *everyone* is fed up with this book and agrees with the anti-linguists out of sheer spite for me. If everyone sincerely believes in what the anti-linguists propose and, for logical consistency, completely renounce every language, modern societies, as we know them, would be impossible; laws, work occupations, socializing, relationships, entertainment, science, infrastructure, and anything that requires interpersonally intelligible communication would evaporate from the realm of possibility in an instant. The complete disregard for all language conventions would be exactly as Hobbes foresaw in a world without a social contract: the "life of a man [everyone]" would be "solitary, poor, nasty, brutish, and short." For there cannot be a society without a foundation on which people implicitly agree, and language is fundamental insofar as even a social contract must be communicated in words people *understand*. If the Tower of Babel were simply an Abrahamic myth, it might as well be real now.

Whether the foundation on which I base my theory is agreeable, liked, plausible, intuitive, common-sensical, or not, there are no shortcuts, be it on paper or in practice, to inquiring about the meaning of life through linguistics.

V

CONCLUSION

We have now reached the final stage of this particular inquiry, yet, ironically, we find ourselves back to the beginning. But I cannot fault myself for having done the required diligence of displacing unfounded, rivaling claims in the philosophy of life, as well as addressing the possibility of outright rejections of my theory beforehand; with all preparations finally behind us, I shall apply all of what was learned in previous chapters to solve the meaning of life.

Due to its legendary importance among philosophers and layfolk alike and the need to meet its mythologized reputation with an answer of equal measure, I now present the lengthiest and most eloquent of chapters . . .

Chapter 6

The Meaning of Life—Solved

I SUBTLY HINTED AND even explicitly indicated on numerous occasions my intention to argue, herein, that the meaning of life is literal. Since it qualifies as a form of meaning, there shall be a number of reasons, other than pragmatic ones presented in the previous chapters, as to why the meaning of life cannot mean anything else but its literal meaning. As we previously saw, the pragmatic reasons thereof are the two *reductiones ad absurdum* that illustrated undesirable consequences of overlooking the use of linguistics when examining a problem; these are consequences that philosophers—no matter how capable—could ever justify as a result of rejecting my answer to the meaning of life. However, this time, I emphasize solutions to the meaning of life instead of emphasizing the consequences of ignoring the common, academic practice of reading its phrase's literal meaning.

The first among my reasons for why 'the meaning of life' is literal has to do with its unusually accommodating grammatical structure. As several philosophers before me had noticed, the first word of the life-problem thereof (i.e., "the") is the very detail that most decisively unravels the mystery of philosophy's greatest problem. However, these observant philosophers thereof, who I mention in the first section below, had not only underestimated the gargantuan influence of the definite article but had also managed to grossly mistake its grammatical usage; as a word deserving much elaboration in its own right, I largely dedicate the first section of this chapter to its explanation and explication. But we shall likewise see much explanation and some explication of the grammar involved of other words forming 'the meaning of life.'

Once the salient grammar rules applying to 'the meaning of life' are out in the open, we shall find that the inquiry will hit an impasse; this is due to each word (forming 'the meaning of life') having multiple semantics that seem to be equally applicable to it. To further supplement the linguistic method and thus disambiguate 'the meaning of life' sufficiently, so that it shall be surely solved, I introduce the ontological puzzles, which were mentioned in chapter 1.

And last, will the answer to the meaning of life overcome nihilism? I leave the reader in suspense.

I

THE DEVIL IS IN THE DETAILS

To solve 'the meaning of life,' we must start with what is easily and surely known of the phrase thereof before inquiring its obscurer details; this begins with spelling out its most salient grammatical details. But the temptation to determine its semantics must be resisted for now.

The reason we cannot yet begin with formally defining the 'the meaning of life' is because its words "meaning" and "life" have multiple nuances of *prima facie* equal applicability. Without an unarbitrary method for discerning the right nuance of key words, we risk destroying the literal boundaries that separate 'the meaning of life' from other phrases, like 'the cat is on the mat.' For instance, we saw in chapters 4–5 how any (arbitrary) stipulation of what constitutes 'meaning' or the (disconcertingly liberal) substitutions of words, e.g., Hepburn's amalgam thesis, eventually leads to perspectival relativism and skepticism. If both perennial problems come back into play, 'the meaning of life' may as well mean virtually anything or absolutely nothing and would, thus, rebecome either relativistic and trivial or meaningless and therefore unsolvable.[1] To prevent the recurrence of skepticism *cum* relativism and the outcomes they entail, we need a process for defining 'the meaning of life' that carries a kindred certainty to '2 + 2 = 4'; this process requires laying bare the grammar of the phrase thereof.

But before I begin with the "easily and surely known" grammatical details of 'the meaning of life,' there is a question worth answering, which, I believe, had already occurred to many readers. Is it really necessary to spell out the grammar of a four-word phrase, which just about anyone fluent with English presumably understands? After all, once philosophical discussions pause and ordinary experiences resume, the ritualistic pretense of hesitation and perplexity toward 'the meaning of life' is superseded by philosophers' thinly disguised overfamiliarity with its individual words. If a philosopher is truly sincere, he would readily—though perhaps begrudgingly—admit that the words 'meaning' and 'life' are inevitable staples in his everyday vocabulary. As for the grammar of 'the meaning of life,' we cannot possibly be as hopelessly incompetent with English as to require a grade-school reminder for how a relatively simple, four-word definite noun phrase works. What revelations about 'the meaning of life' shall we uncover by dutifully deciphering the usages of its determiner, nouns, and preposition? And why must we bother drawing attention to words that we already use with great accuracy? A PhD degree in philosophy carries with it the reasonable presumption that its recipient is very well-acquainted with the language in which he philosophizes. Thus, it is unsurprising why many PhD-wielding philosophers possibly believe the grammatical details of 'the meaning of life' are too primitive and obvious or too unimportant to deign a closer study.

---

1. By "relativistic and trivial," I mean 'the meaning of life' would mean too many different things, which would be true under the perspectival relativism presented in chapter 4. However, the same phrase becomes meaningless when it becomes indistinguishable from other phrases that have nothing to do with the meaning of life. Relativism destroys literal boundaries that keep problems semantically distinct, and skepticism undermines all uncertain claims attempting to replace the loss of the boundaries thereof.

However, if there is anything the literature in the philosophy of life is ever capable of proving, it is that philosophers do not nearly possess an excellent command of words despite their professional prefixes. It is worth repeating from chapter 2, once more, that Baggini stipulated multiple nuances of 'meaning' simultaneously, and Cottingham swapped multiple homonyms of 'life' for a question whose words are obviously in the singular form.

"What is the meaning of life?" is not difficult to understand. But it owes its artificial complexity entirely to the philosophers who are unwilling to fully appreciate how its grammar influences its denotation, since they refuse to consult a dictionary or grammar book. To reuse an example in chapter 1, the convention both aforementioned philosophers violated is plain enough that even a high-school dropout could easily tell the difference between ordering a "coffee" and "coffees"; if this basic sort of language proficiency were not the case for people in general, they would have an even harder time getting by in life. Furthermore, if a polite person clearly orders and pays for *a* cup of coffee, the expectation is for him to receive *one* cup but not none, not two, not three cups of coffee, etc. It is as the well-worn aphorism 'you get what you pay for' implies: the answer to the meaning of life must correspond exactly to how its problem is phrased; if one does not like what 'the meaning of life' entails, one must rephrase the problem rather than becoming like the mythologized Holy Roman Emperor Sigismund by outright assaulting the English language.[2] As a formal study of language—and in this particular case, English—philosophy works best when its participants respect the rules.

In addition to violating the morphology rule concerning singular words "meaning" and "life" in 'the meaning of life,' philosophers had even managed to misuse a third word in the four-word phrase thereof. Below are several instances of more or less the same factually false belief about 'the,' which spread and circulated with impunity in philosophy since 1999:

2. But in rephrasing 'the meaning of life' to an easier problem to solve, the inquirer cannot then claim that he solved the meaning of life, as he had forfeited that privilege in so doing.

The characteristic use of the definite article here suggests that life is presumed to have a single overall purpose and one [*sic.*] which is something we might discover.[3]

[The] placement of the definite article before "meaning" strongly suggests that the question [what is the meaning of life?] is motivated by the assumption that life, or yours and my life, has only a single purpose."[45]

The definite article used in these cases is divorced from any particular empirical context. In empirical contexts, it is used to pick out a particular exemplar out of a class of things, such as "the cat next door" or "the Jew living in the upper apartment." It is used therein as an individuating description to refer to a particular individual out of a class of similar individuals. In both symbolic discourse and philosophy [*sic.*] it is used to refer to a symbolic individual that represents the entire class itself.[6]

The above characterizations of the definite article falter on three counts. First, there is nothing denoted by 'the' that "suggests" "life" in 'the meaning of life' has a *single* purpose, or, to use a few of Lurie's words, *individuates* its object from its "class." A suggestion is optional, but—as being an *analytic truth*—a word and its semantics, e.g., an Oxfordian dictionary definition of 'meaning,' is not a choice and neither is the grammatical usage of 'the.' For example, I cannot *choose* whether or not 'bachelor' means 'an unmarried man' in its applicable context; the "choice" to deny an analytically true statement will result in a self-contradiction, which is always false.[7] Likewise, the "single purpose" that Sharpe, and Seachris

---

3. Sharpe, "In Praise," para. 2.

4. Seachris, *Theism, Naturalism, and Narrative*, 26.

5. Further instances of the same factually false description of the definite article—over the course of eleven years—are found in Seachris' article, "The Meaning of Life as Narrative" (2009), and his co-authored book *What is This Thing Called the Meaning of Life* (2020).

6. Lurie, *Wittgenstein*, 56.

7. A "clever" person could retort that an Ontarian man who marries in Las Vegas is both married and unmarried since Ontario does not recognize Las Vegas marriage certificates; so, we have an example of the concept of

presume is the case is either denoted by 'the meaning of life' or not, but, again, it is no mere suggestion. Second, while "meaning" happens to be single in 'the meaning of life,' it has nothing to do with semantic or grammatical usages of 'the,' as Sharpe, and Seachris mistakenly believe; "meaning" in the phrase thereof is singular because it lacks a certain morpheme, i.e., the affix -*s*, which would have otherwise made it plural, i.e., 'meanings.'

While describing the definite article's grammatical usages, grammarian Sidney Greenbaum in *English Grammar* stated,

> With singular noun phrases [*sic.*] it [the definite article] contrasts with the indefinite article *a /an (a house, the house)*. With plural noun phrases it [the definite article] contrasts the zero article, i.e. the absence of an article or other determiner *(the houses, houses)*, or with the indefinite determiner *some (the houses, some houses)*.[8]

As the name itself implies, the *definite* article makes a *definite* reference. For example, if I were to speak about *the* philosopher, after having just mentioned *Aristotle*, then the definite reference, in this case, is 'Aristotle,' but not 'Socrates,' 'Plato,' or any other philosopher; in this scenario, the nuance of 'the' implied is, "[D]enoting one or more people or things already mentioned or assumed to be common knowledge; the definite article."[9] But the definite article's usages are not limited to singular nouns, since they apply equally to plural nouns, e.g., the houses.

Third, there is nothing in any lexical definition of 'the' that "strongly suggests" that "meaning" in 'the meaning of life' is

---

'bachelor' being contradicted in a particular situation. In response, I could just as well relativize bachelorhood to the state where one is married or to the period wherein his marriage lasts, as well as add other criteria. However, this is unnecessary since the particular instance of states and provinces recognizing and refusing to recognize the same marriage is incommensurable to analytic truths; I only care about the relations of ideas pertaining to the meaning of life. I shall not bother trying to bridge the epistemological gap between matters of fact (being contingent) with relations of ideas (being tautological when applied correctly), since this is an issue beyond the scope of this book.

8. *English Grammar*, 621.

9. *Concise Oxford Dictionary*, 10th ed. (1999), s.v. "the."

interchangeable with any nuance of 'purpose.' If the readers wish to see for themselves what the denotations and grammatical usages of 'the' truly entail, they may browse any respectable dictionary or grammar book written by an actual linguist. But I see no point in listing half a dozen definitions to further prove what should have been common, grade-school knowledge.

Could Sharpe, Seachris, and Lurie reasonably expect that the rules concerning the usages of the definite article will change anytime soon? The short answer is "no." A word's usage is likelier to be removed from English lexicons when English sociolinguistic communities mostly cease using it (e.g., 'evitable'), or a word's usage may change if it is frequently misused (e.g., 'terrific'). According to Peter Norvig, a former director of research at Google, 'the' is by far the most used word in a *massive* sample of English books. Out of 97,565 different words, 'the' accounts for 7.14 percent of a sample size of 743,842,922,321 words, which easily exceeds the word count of a million books combined; the runner-up is 'of' at 4.16 percent.[1011] But apart from Sharpe, Seachris, and Lurie and their gross misunderstandings of the definite article, its usages are not abstruse and 'the' tends to be used more or less correctly by English sociolinguistic communities.[12] As the most used word and the only definite article in the English language, whose roots date as far back as Old English in 900 CE and beyond, 'the' is not changing anytime soon;[13] its change or removal from the English lexicon would be so inconvenient for English sociolinguistic communities that lexicographers would not dare dream of doing either.[14] With the aforesaid facts in mind, my adversaries do not

10. "English Letter Frequency," under title section: Word Counts.

11. Mark Mayzner, who had originally done this sort of research in the early sixties, contacted Norvig for a follow-up study in 2012.

12. I am not implying that using 'the' correctly is the same as knowing how to describe its usages; the former is knowledge-how, and the latter is knowledge-that with respect to the definite article.

13. *Thesaurus*, under title section: What is a *definite article*?

14. To inversely demonstrate the usefulness of the definite article, I challenge naysayers to forgo using it for an entire week. This is not to say it is impossible, but it would add unnecessary effort to speaking and writing English.

have any justification to expediently reinterpret the definite article in 'the meaning of life' other than how it is supposed to be used.

Based on the grammatical blunders presented in this section, we know that if 'the meaning of life' were so obvious a phrase, its details would not have bedeviled *every* philosopher of life to date. Thus, I was warranted in elucidating two grammatical facts of 'the meaning of life,' which I repeat below:

"the" makes a definite reference, and

"meaning" is singular.

By the rules of grammar, these details tell us that 'the meaning of life' makes a specific and a singular reference to "meaning" and determining this reference is what solves the problem thereof; 'the meaning of life' is, after all, a *definite noun phrase*, since it begins with the definite article and has the noun "meaning" immediately following it, so it is entirely about its definite reference. However, we shall see much later that there is another aspect to the answer to the meaning of life and, likewise, another way to state the same answer.

I shall briefly address one last detail, which I have intentionally omitted, before proceeding with semantically disambiguating 'the meaning of life.'

The word whose usage I did not elaborate on is "of" in 'the meaning of life,' but its omission is justified, since it does not alter its phrase's meaning in the way "the" does; the former's only grammatical purpose is to indicate a relationship between two words, and each of its many explicit definitions' applicabilities depends on the nature of the relationship thereof.[15] For example, "of" in "my house is *west* of this coffeeshop" means "expressing the

---

But if one should master such an awkward manner of speaking, that does not imply that others would or would be willing to likewise forgo the definite article's usefulness in everyday conversation.

15. Listing various types of relationships denoted by 'of' would be a considerable waste of space since knowing them neither contributes to solving the meaning of life nor provides insights about it that are not already known.

relationship between a direction and a point of reference."[16] But the aforesaid preposition tells us nothing about my house, other than the direction to its location from a point of reference (i.e., "this coffeeshop"); likewise, "of" in 'the meaning of life' tells us nothing useful about "meaning." If I could define "of" as of this very moment, it would presuppose knowing what "meaning" semantically means, which is, as of now, question-begging; it would imply the meaning of life is already solved. So, the meaning of "of" in 'the meaning of life' is unnecessary for my purpose herein and redundant once my purpose is achieved.

We have temporarily reached the limits of the linguistic method by adumbrating the most salient features of grammar. I turn to elaborate this "process for defining 'the meaning of life' that carries a certainty kindred to '2 + 2 = 4,'" as stated near the beginning of this section.

II

ONTOLOGICAL PUZZLES

Given the facts that "the" in 'the meaning of life' makes a definite reference, and "meaning" is morphologically singular, there can only be one nuance of 'meaning' that necessarily applies to the phrase thereof; these facts are analytical truths based on inbuilt principles, which are necessary for the English language to remain intelligible for its rule-abiding participants.[17] So, we are indeed

16. *Concise Oxford Dictionary*, 10th ed. (1999), s.v. "of."

17. If the reader is still wondering why these facts are analytic truths: imagine one instance where "the" in 'the meaning of life' does not make a definite reference or "meaning" is plural. In the imagined instance, where either fact is contradicted, does it have any truth? If a contradiction is always false, then it is an impossibility.

Consider, once again, the implications of what is described in great detail in chapter 5. What happens when the conventions of the English language are dismissed? As we saw, the English language, and any society whose institutions depend on it, cannot function if its principles become mere suggestions; the first thing lost is interpersonal intelligibility (i.e., we cannot understand others and cannot be understood by them) and, later, institutions that are vital to the

assured of an indubitable and definitive starting point for solving the meaning of life. By figuring out the meaning of "meaning" in 'the meaning of life,' we shall finally be in a position to discern how to non-arbitrarily define the meaning of "life" in the next section. Both words represent different aspects of the same answer to the problem thereof, but "meaning" constrains how "life" means.

The definite reference, which definitively solves the meaning of life in the first of its two aspects, is known once a few ontological puzzles are solved herein, but first a reminder. Does the reader remember Aristotle's example in chapter 1, wherein 'two' necessarily presumes a 'one'? An ontological priority occurs whenever an entity's existence necessarily implies the existence of another. Consider the following examples: first, the existence of one molecule of water presupposes the existences of at least two atoms of hydrogen and one of oxygen; it is possible for hydrogen and oxygen to exist without water, but it is impossible for water to exist without at least two atoms of hydrogen and one of oxygen. Ergo, the latter two elements are ontologically prior to a molecule of water. Second, the existence of a human presupposes that at least one mammal exists or existed. To be clear: if the human in question is the only one of his species and dies, it does not necessarily imply the extinction of mammals. But if all mammals die, then there cannot be a single human alive, since the latter is a member of the former, but not the converse. Hence, be it the animal or concept, 'mammal' is ontologically prior to 'human.' Third, and more relevantly, a symbol, such as a word, presupposes that a reference is being made; whether or not the reference itself exists is irrelevant for the ontological priority to occur, e.g., 'Pegasus,' the winged horse.

---

functioning of societies shall cease. For example, there cannot be any laws, commerce, infrastructure, education, etc. without a means for individuals to communicate intelligibly. Lest we aspire to return to the Stone Age, there cannot be an exception to the most basic principles of the English language (e.g., morphologically singular words). There is no room for a needlessly argumentative debate, especially while the setting is formal, academic, but not colloquial, and, therefore, reliant on the very language whose importance philosophers are attempting to minimize and undermine.

An instance contrary to the third example above is a person's pareidolic perception of a "face" on a floor tile. Similar to philosophers' imaginative opinions of the meaning of life, coincidental contrasts of color, shapes, and lighting, giving the appearance of a face, are too ambiguous to be an actual representation of it. Whereas a painting of a face is not pareidolia; it is a deliberate attempt by its artist to have his audience recognize his portrayal of a face. But even if the face portrayed in a painting is of a fictional person, it still counts as a symbol that signifies a face. Likewise, what differentiates a written, English word from unintelligible markings on a surface is the former's belonging to the English language; as I wrote in chapter 5, the purpose of English is for its participants to be understood and understand others. In all the above examples, if the ontologically necessary entity in question does not exist, then neither can the entities that presuppose its existence exist. I shall apply Aristotle's ontological priority through the following two ontological puzzles. If the reader so desires, they may read the leading question of the following two paragraphs and try to figure out the answers before I give them away in the following sentences.

Whenever a person reads, hears, or thinks, "What is the meaning of life?", what is the very first thing that must occur for the question thereof to be meaningfully and relevantly answered? When electromagnetic waves impress themselves upon our retinae, and acoustic waves travel through colliding air molecules and onto our eardrums, our afferent nerves process them as experiences through tens of billions of electrochemical impulses; whether our contemplation of the meaning of life came as a result of reading or hearing about it, *something* extremely subtle, yet no less significant, is happening amid all these synapses. What is it that differentiates the printed words 'the meaning of life' from a scribbled drawing by a 5-year-old child or its utterance from cacophonies of second-rate "music" at a nightclub? How is 'the meaning of life' not a nonsensical phrase? When groups of printed symbols read as 'the meaning of life,' or when someone utters "the meaning of life," something must occur for these symbols to mean something to someone; if we take away the ontologically prior, neurogenic occurrence of that "something," 'the meaning of life' would strike us as just another unintelligible visual experience or meaningless noise. However, this is clearly not the case as there is a reason 'the meaning of life' often elicits genuine curiosity, whereas Chomsky's "[c]olorless green ideas sleep furiously" does not.[18] As the attentive reader already knows or should know by now, *that "something" that must occur* has to do with the literal meaning of 'the meaning of life'; the person in question must understand "what is the meaning of life?" in order to answer it meaningfully and relevantly. But there is a little more to this story.

What is the very thing that makes any thought or discussion about the meaning of life ontologically possible? For 'the meaning of life' to be contemplated or discussed, it must have literal meaning; if the phrase thereof lacks literal meaning, then based on its grammar (which I had repeatedly demonstrated), it cannot mean anything at all. However, there is an obvious difference between a person's *understanding* of the literal meaning and *literal meaning per se*, which is still worth mentioning. 'The meaning of life' does not ontologically depend on any individual person's understanding of it; if someone never heard of 'the meaning of life' or misunderstood it, it shall not cease to be a meaningful phrase. Whereas literal meaning is necessary for 'the meaning of life' to be meaningful. It is therefore important for my readers to remember the aforementioned distinction, so as to avoid confusion while I discuss both ontological priorities.

'Literal' is defined as "taking words in their usual or most basic sense without metaphor or allegory,"[19] and, depending on the context, 'meaning' may denote either of the following,

1. "what is meant by a word, text, concept, or action,"[20] and

2. "worthwhile quality; purpose."[21]

18. *Syntactic Structures*, 15.
19. *Concise Oxford Dictionary*, 10th ed. (1999), s.v. "literal."
20. *Concise Oxford Dictionary*, 10th ed. (1999), s.v. "meaning."
21. *Concise Oxford Dictionary*, 10th ed. (1999), s.v. "meaning."

There are, of course, a few more lesser-known definitions of 'meaning,' which could also be quoted, but their relevance is nil, as the context I set leaves no room for ambiguity. Since "literal" is prefixed to "meaning" and semantically modifies it, (1) is the nuance of 'meaning' that must apply. For if we were to disregard (1) as being applicable to "meaning" in 'literal meaning,' a semantic contradiction would ensue; as 'literal' is defined above, it requires a 'meaning' that is congruent with "taking words in their usual or most basic sense without metaphor or allegory." (1) involves "what is meant by a word, text…", which semantically agrees with what 'literal' denotes; whereas other nuances of 'meaning' do not. So, any homonym of 'meaning,' other than (1), is literally impossible for "meaning" in 'literal meaning,' which is ontologically prior to 'the meaning of life.' To be clear, references (e.g., literal meaning) are ontologically prior to symbols (e.g., 'the meaning of life'). A symbol can only be considered a 'symbol' insofar as it has a reference; without a reference, a mark or a sound cannot be a symbol, since it does not signify anything. Therefore, the meaning of life is necessarily literal.

However, what would happen if an anti-linguist insists that he retains the "power" to disregard the literal meaning of 'the meaning of life' anyway? Keep in mind that, as educated, English-speaking adults, each one of us has used many thousands of English words many thousands of times; so, the act of disregarding any literal meaning, however imperfect our knowledge of words and their usages are, is as hard as making a conscious effort to stop breathing.[22] Even if, through strenuous dedication, one resists thinking about their literal meanings each time he reads or hears words, he will most likely resume in thinking literally, as if gasping voraciously for air; the alternative is that, by forgoing any literal contemplation of its words each time they appear before him, his

22. If I were pressed for exactly how literal meaning differs in a person's thoughts compared to the contents of dictionaries, I say, if the latter were a person, then the former would be akin to a "stick" figure drawing of that person; our mental grasps of words' literal meanings are extremely limited, and they usually work as an association of experiences between the sound of a signifying word and our encounters with physical objects or words it signifies.

ability to understand the English language will worsen without practice until he becomes illiterate. But for the rest of us who lack such a Camusian disdain for conventions and the Sisyphean dedication to constantly avoid what is as involuntary as breathing while one sleeps: literal thoughts are inevitable. Once light reaches the retinae, and the printed symbol 'the meaning of life' appears before a person whose primary language is English, he consciously realizes it no sooner than he grasps its literal meaning; after all, the synapses, which make up our thoughts, travel as quickly as 120 meters per second.

As synapses begin and electrochemical impulses pass from one neuronal membrane to the next, the experience of seeing dried markings of ink are impulsively transformed into the words of one's personal semantics and vocabulary. It is to say, we are as aware of this symbol-generating or symbol-pairing mental activity inasmuch as a writer is witting of the exact symbol and location of each button on his computer's keyboard while his eyes are shut. Were it not for our previous, tacit knowledge of the words 'the,' 'meaning,' 'of,' and 'life,' the transformation of dried ink markings into something meaningful cannot occur. But unlike struggling with learning how to use 'withal' in a sentence, the words composing 'the meaning of life' are easy enough that virtually every person whose primary language is English understands them sufficiently. So, while one could find it moot that a lay person's literal understanding of 'withal' is second nature, the same is most likely untrue of his literal grasp of 'the meaning of life.'

I have now solved the meaning of life by demonstrating that—first—a person must understand what a question literally means before he is *epistemically* able to answer it relevantly and meaningfully; perhaps, the more suitable term for this "ontological priority" is 'epistemic priority.' Thus, we may say there is a linguistic *knowledge requirement* for answering "what is the meaning of life?" meaningfully and relevantly; whereas asserting the contrary is question-begging, since we cannot properly answer a question whose words we do not know. Second, for a person to understand what a question literally means, the question thereof must be literally meaningful. As a literally meaningful phrase that can only have one, specific meaning, the meaning of life must be literal meaning, and the same is true of the phrase in question form: "What is the meaning of life?" By contrast, if we supposed it references any meaning other than the literal meaning, 'the meaning of life,' by its own grammatical stipulations, would strike us as unintelligible markings on paper (or noise, if spoken); it has no room for multiple meanings or any meaning but the one it specifically references, which renders it intelligible. So, as a literally meaningful phrase, 'the meaning of life' necessarily presupposes the very meaning that makes it intelligible, *Q.E.D.*

I turn to the second aspect of the answer to 'the meaning of life.' When we know the full nature of literal meaning, I shall, at last, be sufficiently prepared to confront the threat of meaninglessness, which is infamously known as 'nihilism.'

III

LITERAL MEANING, CATEGORY, AND REFERENCE

At the beginning of this book, I promised my readers that I shall not be another philosopher to take for granted my uses of "meaning," so I shall dutifully explain it in lucid detail. By "literal meaning," there is no mystical entity, like flowing, transparent waves of magic or an obese, old man in a white beard jerking his fingers from Heavenly clouds above to grant life meaning; instead, it usually appears in the form of dried ink markings on paper, pixels on a screen, or soundwaves in a discernible pattern. The medium that enables these patterns to reach our sensoria is either through electromagnetic waves, in the form of radiation, or through the collision of particles that we call "sound."[23] These symbols, printed (in a book), pixelated (on a computer screen), or audible (through oral conversation), correspond to other printed, pixelated, or audible symbols in a certain way; this sort of inter-symbolic

---

23. Alternatively, there is Braille, which is one example of a third medium, involving touch, for the transmission of literal meaning.

correspondence is typically known as an 'explicit definition.' Inter-symbolic correspondences have to do with symbols signifying each other in an endless cycle or a gargantuan, circular loop of references; yes, English semantics references itself, and its explanation amounts to circular reasoning, but this is in fact how English works. In short, semantics, of which all literal meanings are part, is basically a web of tens of thousands of inter-defining English words. And words' literal meanings are represented in one of several forms (e.g., collections of letters represented by markings of dried ink).

With the above descriptions in mind, it is clear that semantics, of which literal meanings are part, is far too broad an answer to be informatively true of 'the meaning of life.' For example, if a Canadian were to ask me, "Where do you live?" and I respond, "I live in Canada," I am being rather general about my whereabouts, even while my answer is true; after all, thirty-eight million Canadians live here too. Likewise, for phrases wherein "meaning" immediately follows "the," e.g., 'the meaning of car,' it is often the case that literal meaning is ontologically prior to other meanings;[24] this is to say, many (but not all) definite noun phrases share the same ontological priority as 'the meaning of life.' However—returning to my initial example—if I clarified that I live in the Province of Ontario, assuming I am speaking to an Ontarian in Ontario, the answer would still be too vague. Although it is not advisable that I answer by giving the name of the street on which I live, I would be answering the question perfectly. Does the prior example mean "what is the meaning of life?" could be answered less vaguely?

---

24. A counterexample to phrases beginning with 'the meaning' being of literal meaning is "what is the meaning of your drawing?" In this case, the possessive pronoun "your" prevents its corresponding phrase from being a literal-meaning reference like 'the meaning of life.' Thus, the reference of "meaning" in 'the meaning of your drawing' is too ambiguous for its literal meaning to have an ontological priority.

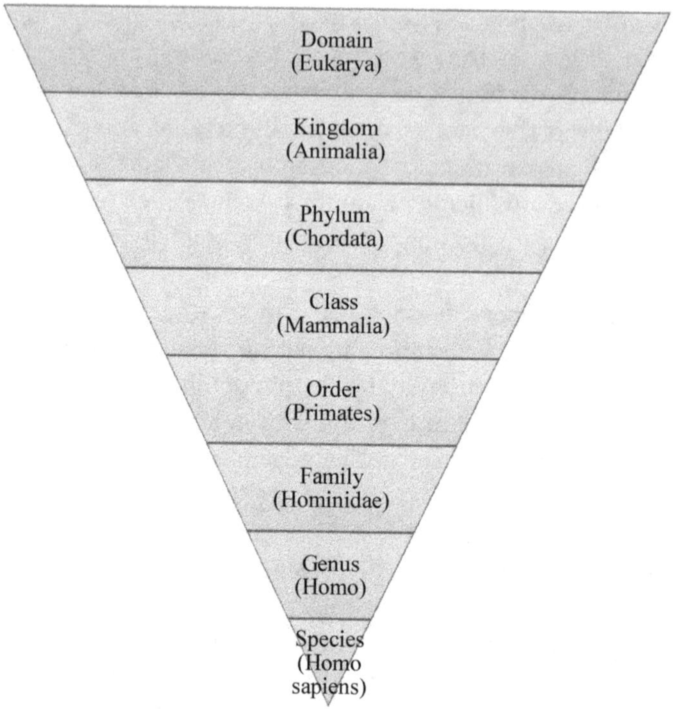

Figure 3. The above represents an inverted pyramid of a human's taxonomy.

To put aspects of the answer to the meaning of life into perspective, consider the inverted taxonomy pyramid in figure 3. If someone is *human*, then his belonging in all the categories of figure 3 is analytically entailed; he is at once a eukaryote, animal, vertebrate, mammal, primate, and hominid, and of the *Homo* genus and *Homo* sapiens species. However, if Professor Susan Dimock were asked by Professor Jagdish Hattiangadi, "Who are you?", it would be rather strange for the former to reply, "I am a eukaryote"; we would expect her to introduce herself with her name. Aside from it being normally impolite, even if Dimock replied less ambiguously and said, "I am human," she has not done enough to differentiate herself from the other eight billion members of her species. As is hardly worthy of mention, the higher we go on the inverted pyramid, the more inclusive and general the category becomes, and thus the answer becomes less informative.

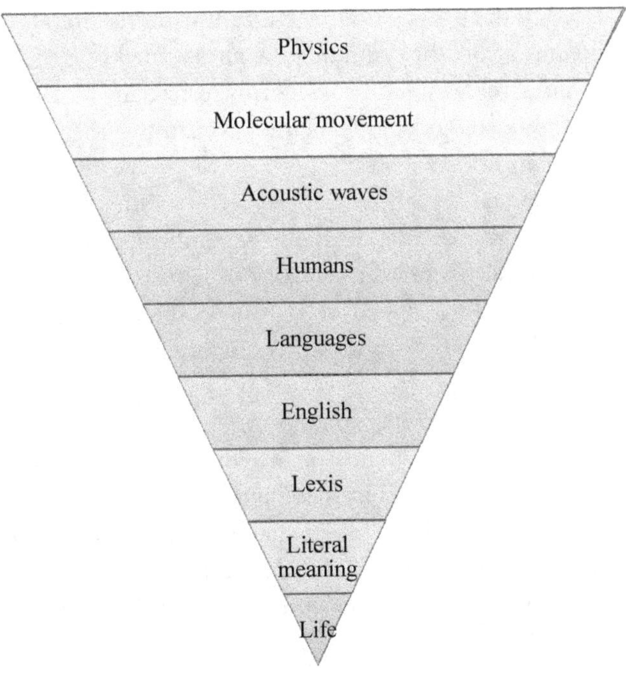

Figure 4. The above represents an inverted pyramid of a "taxonomy" of the meaning of life.

Similar to human taxonomy, we see that, according to figure 4, 'the meaning of life' is at once literally meaningful, a collection of words, an English phrase, and of a language created by humans; furthermore, we know that partaking in any language, such as speaking, reading, or thinking, is done physically, and therefore explainable by physics.[25] But with everything said, there is an

25. However, for the sake of clarity, this does not mean abstract sciences are physical, simply because they are transmitted physically, e.g., through vocal apparatuses. 'The meaning of life' remains an abstraction.

important respect in which Dimock claiming that she is human, for example, differs from describing 'the meaning of life' as being literal or a subset of semantics; the latter claim is vague but it is not as vague as the former or as vague as claiming that 'the meaning of life' is an English phrase or a phonetic pattern of sounds. As demonstrated in the first section, 'the meaning of life' literally references "meaning." So, the claim that the phrase thereof is of literal meaning is not irrelevant, and considering, especially, the general perplexity of philosophers of life, neither is claiming 'the meaning of life is literal' uninformative.

Since 'the meaning of life' is necessarily its literal meaning, we know that its word "life," as being semantically modified by "meaning," must fall within the category of semantics. As the category encompassing all English words' official definitions, semantics *per se* is indiscriminate about which nuance applies to "life" in 'the meaning of life.'

So, how do we tell which nuance of 'life' applies to "life" in 'the meaning of life'? It depends on whether the nuance of 'life' is explicitly stated or implied by a context that narrows the list of homonyms. If no nuance of 'life' is made explicit, then the next best means of disambiguating "life" in 'the meaning of life' is by finding the context; if neither is applicable, then the phrase 'the meaning of life' cannot mean anything specifically other than a general category of meaning (i.e., semantics) until a nuance of 'life' is selected.

Usually, a context may be apparent by the larger body of text in which 'the meaning of life' is found; alternatively, the physical setting or place where the phrase is mentioned could sometimes provide context. For example, in a biology classroom, 'life' most likely means "the condition that distinguishes animals and plants from inorganic matter, including the capacity for growth, functional activity, and continual change preceding death."[26] In a place of prayer, like a mosque, or if someone is implicitly referring to himself, 'life' could mean "the existence of an individual human

---

26. *Concise Oxford Dictionary*, 10th ed. (1999), s.v. "life."

being or animal."[27] Of a lively party, it may be said 'life' means "vitality, vigour; or energy."[28] While 'the meaning of life' is a different phrase each time its semantics differ, their meanings are always the same because the category of meaning they ontologically presuppose is context-independent.

Semantics represents the categorical aspect of the answer to the meaning of life, whereas the contextual aspect represents the process by which a homonym of 'life' is made applicable to "life." In a type-token-tone framework, then, the type of meaning that applies to 'the meaning of life' is always literal, and it includes all its tokens (i.e., definitions); the applicable token is a single nuance of 'life' selected from literally meaningful homonyms, and the tone is the context determining which token applies to "life" in the phrase thereof. Given the reasoning above, every discussion of the meaning of life requires a context; if the reader wants to know the meaning of life non-arbitrarily, an explicit definition of 'life' or a definition-limiting context should immediately follow any mention of 'the meaning of life.' For example, if someone asks me, "What is the meaning of life?", my immediate response is, "What do you mean by 'life'?" If the person asking the former answers my question satisfactorily, then he immediately solves the meaning of life; should the person thereof meet the qualifying semantics of "life," then his life is meaningful, whether he believes it or not. However, if the person does not know the words forming the question he asks, then his utterance of 'the meaning of life' does not acquire a context-specific literal meaning; thus, in that instance, wherein 'the meaning of life' appears, no nuance of 'life' is specifically attributable to "life." It should be noted that once "life" in 'the meaning of life' is semantically determined, its nuance cannot be swapped for another, lest one desires to inquire about a semantically different problem with identical words. But if the desire to inquire about a different problem with identical words is the case, the person (e.g., Cottingham) making the swap must be clear about it in order to avoid unnecessary equivocation.

27. *Concise Oxford Dictionary*, 10th ed. (1999), s.v. "life."
28. *Concise Oxford Dictionary*, 10th ed. (1999), s.v. "life."

The attentive reader now knows both its categorical and contextual aspects and why the former aspect of the answer to the meaning of life is apodictically true and unchanging; if there is any lingering doubt about its truth, the reader may as well reread this book in as few sittings as possible, without speed-reading or taking extended breaks. (When in doubt, I strongly recommend the use of a respectable dictionary—even if the word in question seems simple—as it had been invaluable in my case.)

With the nature of "meaning" in 'the meaning of life' known, I am now in an informed position to address the last problem for this book, which is the threat of meaninglessness.

IV

INTERSUBJECTIVITY VERSUS ELVES

Since I have definitively solved the meaning of life, and its meaning is necessarily literal, I shall mainly discuss 'nihilism' and 'objectivity' insofar as they affect the reality of the semantics of 'the meaning of life.' For it would be pointless to discuss other aspects of objectivity, which affect other kinds of meaning that involve theories of life I had refuted. As far as I know, objective semantics has no proponents in the philosophy of life, but I shall argue against it anyway while denying its rejection implies nihilism; the theory I advance is, after all, new and so is the discussion of its implications.

Nihilism is the denial that life has any objective meaning. Conversely, the meaning of life is said to be objectively meaningful when a realist claims the existence of its semantics is completely mind-independent; for example, if no one—not just one person but everyone—ever thought about the meaning of life, 'life' would still be objectively meaningful. If the former is true, and 'life' is objectively meaningless, then it does not matter whether the answer to the meaning of life is proven apodictically true or not; if the meaning in question is merely conventional, e.g., an agreement for how words should be used, its indubitability does not necessarily mean it is objective (or exists outside of convention). One way to better understand whether nihilism or objective meaning is true of the meaning of life is by answering the following question. Did we create literal meaning, or did we discover it?

As a phrase that is necessarily of its literal meaning, the meaning of life must be intersubjectively meaningful, rather than objectively so; that is to say, many humans, over the course of many years, agreed on what sounds and perceptible symbols count as words and what they should mean, but they did not discover semantics; even the many loanwords the English language owes to other languages were ultimately created by agreed-upon stipulations. So, the phrase 'the meaning of life' and its semantics were likewise created. For if humans had otherwise discovered semantics, then the meanings of words cannot be said to have evolved or possessed histories that etymology tracks; semantics would instead be eternal, indestructible, and mind-independent, and, thus, objective, as a realist is expected to argue.

But semantic realism raises worse problems than the threat of nihilism, which results from claiming that humans created semantics. First, if I were to adopt semantic realism, I risk trading nihilism for skepticism by claiming that 'the meaning of life' has objective semantics while failing to prove it is *necessarily* the case. As I stated in the first chapter, "[A] skeptic only needs a crucial proposition within a valid argument to have a *single* possibility of being false in order to undermine its conclusion's truth-certainty"; this includes the uncertainty of whether a word is indeed objectively meaningful or mistaken for one. The only way to defeat skepticism is to remove any possibility for a claim to be false so that there would be nothing for a skeptic to doubt; the semantic realist needs to advance relevant analytic truths that prove 'the meaning of life' indubitably possesses objective semantics. However, analytic truths are useless if the thing in question remains to be explained; other than being mind-independent, we shall see that 'objectivity' is an inchoate concept, whose favorable claims are unwarranted. Second, semantic realism lacks veracity; after all, it contradicts etymological evidence that proves semantics, among other things, are in fact created by humans.

While skepticism is an insufficient reason for rejecting it, semantic realism's lack of veracity, as a result of contradicting etymology, gives sufficient reason.[29] But even if semantic realism should not be rejected for the aforementioned reason, it would be self-defeating on the basis that its claims favoring objective meaning are unwarranted and inherently nonsensical. Since too little is known about objective meaning, it would be impossible to refute it without knowing whether it entails any patent contradiction, and I know of none. So, if semantic realism should be defeated, it requires raising concerns about how philosophers had come to believe objectivity exists, i.e., whether such beliefs are epistemically warranted or not. But objectivity's reverence among philosophers makes its rejection quite controversial, since it is a concept that had deeply entrenched itself in philosophy since at least as early as the writings of Plato. Therefore, I shall advance an obviously absurd claim, which lacks the famousness of objectivity but shares its justificatory flaws; this way, the absurd claim thereof is easier to examine neutrally, and I shall argue that its rejection *mutatis mutandis* applies to objectivity. Furthermore, if claims favoring the existence of objectivity are epistemically impossible, then I further argue that any claim favoring the opposite of objectivity—nihilism—is likewise nonsensical and unfounded; after all, adding or subtracting 'o' from a number shall neither increase nor decrease its value, which is what I seek to prove with objectivity and nihilism vis-à-vis the meaning of life.

With the aforementioned strategies in mind, let us imagine a scenario wherein 'objective meaning' is swapped with the belief that many elves inhabit the Earth. The sole purpose of elves is to watch over humans and perform various deeds to bestow utmost happiness upon our species. Like objective meaning, elves

29. If we reject semantic realism on the sole basis of entailing skepticism, then we would have to reject every dubitable claim, including those made by science, which is impracticable; it would thus be prudent to find a stronger reason for its rejection.

are imperceptible; the specifics of their deeds are beyond our comprehension and irreducible to physics, and no human could confidently assert he had once encountered one (because they are imperceptible). But we may know of them indirectly. For example, when a person's mood inexplicably changes for the better, it is metaphysically possible that an elf caused it, even while the person in question fails to realize it. 'Elf realism,' as I call it, is contrasted by the claim that elves do not exist because there is no such thing as 'utmost happiness.'

Did I manage to convince the reader to believe in elf realism or, for the lack of utmost happiness, its denial? 54 percent of Icelanders believe me;[30] as a matter of fact, there have been costly road construction projects either stopped, delayed, or altered with Icelanders looking to avoid disrupting the habitat of invisible elves.[31] So, perhaps my elf realism is not so absurd after all. But if elf realism is still unbelievable, it is because the reader had just witnessed me fabricate a belief backed by insufficient justification or evidence; it matters not how many people believe in elf realism or—more to the point—how many philosophers espouse one form of objectivity or another. Put simply: if a claim is unwarranted, then it is nonsense. But before anyone should dismiss elf realism, it is worth noting that philosophy professes to treat beliefs by their merit rather than their popularity. Given the similarities between both concepts, if we assume philosophers are without undue bias, then elf realism should receive the same care and attention from its opponents and proponents as objectivity does. After all, philosophy evaluates or should evaluate claims based on merit, not those that appeal to the majority.

As we saw with elf realism, the idea of 'objectivity' originated with its first mention in a document written by *someone*; whether the individual in question is Plato, Pythagoras, or someone unknown, it is irrelevant. If a claim introduced by someone is non-analytic and, thus, not self-evidently true, then the person originating it must meet its burden of proof by demonstrating how

30. Warren, "Iceland Believes in Elves."
31. Wainwright, "Respect the Elves."

he came to know of it. So, if I owe an explanation for how I came to believe elves exist, then whoever argues for semantic objectivity must do the same.

As humans with epistemic limitations, our knowledge ultimately derives from two sources: observation and language; either a claim is empirical and observation-based or analytic and language-based. Therefore, if a belief in the existence of objective semantics is warranted, then it must be either observation-based or language-based.

However, like the elves I imagined, the objectivity that makes semantics mind-independent is not observable. This means that we cannot sedate a living human, dissect his body, and observe the instantiation of an objectively meaningful life therein; objective meaning cannot be tasted, touched, smelled, or seen, and it does not emit any sound and does not have mass or energy. So, objective meaning is not something discoverable through observation-based sciences.

Neither is what is claimed of objective meaning language-based. For as we have seen in the previous sections, markings of dried ink, pixels on a screen, and sounds cannot transform into literally meaningful words without at least one mind existing to perceive them; without any minds, literal meaning would be reduced to meaningless, physically manifest markings or noises, but nothing more. However, 'objective meaning' is by definition 'mind-independent,' which means that the thing that supposedly makes semantics "objective" cannot inhere in the physical manifestations of language, i.e., dried ink markings, pixels, sound, or our thoughts.[32] So, the most characteristic description of 'objectivity' contradicts the mind-dependence of language symbols, which acquire meaning while being perceived by at least one mind.[33]

32. The physical manifestation of thoughts can be known in a limited way, such as through neuroimaging.

33. When I say the English language is mind-dependent, I do not mean it is dependent on any individual mind; it is dependent on all minds capable of affecting its usage. This means that if someone misunderstands 'the meaning of life,' the phrase thereof shall not have an altered meaning. However, if linguists gather together in agreement and stipulate replacing the old semantics for

But if it were instead claimed that 'objectivity' is analytically true of semantics—somehow—then it would be question-begging; what has yet to be proven as "objective" is being assumed as the case while being actively perceived by a mind. In other words, we cannot think outside our thoughts and see if the semantics in question continue to subsist while we are not thinking about it; thus, given our epistemic limitations for coming to know what we know, the idea of "mind-independence" is vague because it is incoherent and unintelligible.

Like my story about elves, the claim that there is such thing as objective semantics must meet a burden of proof; there must be some way that its first-ever proponent had come to know of whatever it is that makes semantics objective. But since the few ways in which we acquire knowledge cannot be attributed to objectivity, we must reject the mythic ideal as being as imaginary and unwarranted as the claim that elves exist.

Neither is it reasonable to assume that our minuscule size in the vast universe or the relatively short time we live causes our lives to be ultimately meaningless; living eternally as giants would still not make anyone's life any more meaningful than it already is. Unlike the universe and other objects of temporal or physical greatness, we are conscious, living things capable of thought, feelings, desires, innovation, among other things, that the universe is not; in other words: size does not matter. The often-repeated wonder of how insignificant we are when compared to larger or longer-lasting objects is as nonsensical as claiming that the lack of happiness comes as a result of the inexistence of elves. But make no mistake, even if we explored the entire universe, we cannot meaningfully say that objectivity does not exist; from an epistemic perspective, empirically warranting such claim, for example, would require visiting—what I call—the "realm of inexistence" and confirming that objectivity indeed resides among "inexistent entities," which is impossible; inexistent entities are impossible to

---

the words 'the meaning of life' with new ones, they might succeed. The above descriptions are what I have in mind for my latest use of "mind-dependence."

confirm as inexistent because it is in its very definition itself: they do not manifest at all.

We are the ones who invented the concept of 'meaning,' and the mere addition of an idea or the lack thereof does not change the meaningfulness of the life lived or life at present. Once the man-made concept of 'meaning' became a tradition, our lives henceforth acquired conventional meaning, whether we believe or like it or not. The idea of 'nihilism' or the lack of objective *meaning*—for a word whose nature cannot be anything other than intersubjective—is, therefore, a quaint fiction, popularized by someone, possibly Gorgias, who probably died in antiquity; without the word 'meaning,' there simply cannot be meaning, and, insofar as it is a word, it is part of a convention, e.g., the English language. The first mention of 'objective meaning,' and its related cognates, is tantamount to introducing an idea that adds *perceived* value and claiming that its absence subtracts a value that never subsisted; nihilism's effect on life is therefore equivalent to subtracting 'o' from a number and does not result in an actual difference or a negative value. Thus, our lives cannot be "nihilistic" insofar as meaning had always existed in the minds of humans as a semantically meaningful word and cannot subsist from without.

If any living thing qualifies as a reference of the word 'life,' then its life cannot fail to have meaning; after all, we are collectively the masters who created the rules of languages and their semantics, including the ideas of 'meaning' and 'life' of English semantics.

V

GRAND CONCLUSION

I have completely fulfilled my promises by providing the definitive answer to the meaning of life, demonstrating its truth apodictically, and explaining and explicating—in exceptionally lucid details—the nature of the answer thereof. However, the unmentioned Herculean implications of the answer to the meaning of life are easy to miss because of their equally impressive subtlety. So, in the place of the usual, lackluster regurgitation, befitting of mediocre philosophy books, I shall conclude mine by adumbrating potentially surprising outcomes of what the answer to the meaning of life entails.

First, my theory of life's certainty offers its knowers an unparalleled comfort against the infamous perennial problems of philosophy, such as skepticism, relativism, and nihilism, which are corrosive and toxic to one's overall confidence; it is the sort of comfort obtained only in knowing something for certain, which is most often seen in mathematics and classical logic. But even if my adversaries should persistently disregard the absolute truths I painstakingly established, I had gone further in demonstrating that any alternative to my answer is impracticable, aside from it being veridically impossible; the practical scenarios I constructed in chapters 4 and 5 illustrate that there cannot be the possibility of agreement without a shared and consistently followed medium for communication, such as English. Therefore, the aforementioned answer is not only theoretically perfect in being absolute and plentifully detailed, but it also reflects indispensably in practice; for without the English language's rules, in which 'the meaning of life' is inextricably embedded, we ultimately risk losing our most valuable type of medium (i.e., shared languages) for conveying information intelligibly. Whereas the theories I refuted had offered no guarantees that their answers to the meaning of life are necessarily the case and, thus, offer no assurance against looming threats of skepticism, relativism, and nihilism. Instead of the coolness of analytic truths and attentiveness to the original problem, my adversaries had myopically relied upon the ostentatious force of charisma and bias-confirmation drawn from nonfactual and speculative arguments favoring popular beliefs.

Second, I maintained neutrality throughout my book by basing my answer on the original question while refusing to speculate or subscribe to any popular belief about the meaning of life. But even as the meaning of life's answer had become increasingly apparent with the passing chapters, I had steadfastly withheld my answer until I was sure its introduction was completely necessitated and warranted. Conversely, my adversaries had deemphasized the literal meaning of "what is the meaning of life?" and had proceeded to answer it without its closer reading; however, the few philosophers who indeed noticed a detail or two had failed to do minimal research and, thus, had blundered in describing well-known facts about grammar. But there may be one downside to my theory: its explanatory success and potential. Philosophers may reject my method of inquiry because it risks upending millennia of aimless, speculative inquiries, which seldom and haphazardly bore fruits, especially if the status quo benefits their careers and their literary corpora.

Third, in maintaining neutrality, it, therefore, became possible for my inquiry to acquire scientific fidelity; as I had just mentioned, my theory threatens traditional philosophies because its method actually brings results. As I stated in the preface of my book, I discarded multiple theories I once regarded as true of the meaning of life upon finding evidence proving otherwise; in this case, the science that applies to 'the meaning of life' is linguistics. By contrast, my opponents conflated distinct sciences by assuming the inability of one (i.e., physics) to explain 'the meaning of life' is a strike against other scientific explanations (i.e., linguistics), as we saw with Tolstoy, and Cottingham. But even those who happened to notice linguistics had still dismissed its insights without understanding it and without sufficient reason.

Fourth, my theory of life has distinguished itself from those of Wolf, and Craig by refusing to exclude lives, by proclaiming them meaningless, through arbitrary stipulations or by playing favorites with normative beliefs or religion; in other words, there is no elitism to be found or any command for which activities, beliefs, preferences, attitudes, or any living circumstance that must be performed or attained for life to be meaningful. Under my scientifically observant theory of life, each living thing's life is inalienably meaningful if it is referenced by a nuance of 'life' in the phrase 'the meaning of life.' The only requirement for a life to have the meaning of life is for a person to be referenceable by the word 'life'; this criterion is neutral insofar as it indiscriminately applies to all living creatures.

Fifth, I had taken every precaution to consistently name the very problem I set out to solve, and I defined, explained, and explicated it transparently and in nauseatingly lucid detail. Whereas the theories throughout the philosophy of life, whether they are as eloquent as the writings of Cottingham and Baggini or as forceful as Craig's, leave important details for readers to figure out on their own.

Sixth, what do the readers gain from learning about the definitive answer to the meaning of life? Instead of mellifluous ideals, which are unlikely life-changing, we have already reaped the rewards of the meaning of life in being able to use the word 'life' and its embedded ideas.

Although it is hard to appreciate what we already possess—for we are by nature insatiably greedy—its absence would be noticed by virtually everyone, as if a neglected, old friend had departed. 'Life' is a prominent participant in our vocabularies that contributes to the wealth of English expressions. Hidden in plain sight, we overlook what is so familiar and seamless while it contiously molds our enigmatic views of ourselves and others; we frequently use 'life' and talk about our historical existences, everyday feelings, desire for change, preferences, health, death, etc. Unlike the abandoned offspring of many relatively "successful" theories that, once written or read, are stowed away into the background of one's mind, only to be forgotten, 'life' is our constant companion; for we cannot technically live without it if we do not have the vocabulary to express it.

While philosophy is not known for its assurances but, rather, infamous for its uncertainties, the readers now know at least one truth that no skeptic, relativist, or nihilist could ever wrest from them; unregretfully, I had sacrificed many years of my life so that you may know for certain the meaning of yours.

Bibliography

Adams, E. M. "The Meaning of Life." *International Journal for Philosophy and Religion* 51 (2002) 71–81. https://www.doi.org/10.1023/A:1014465302653.

Aristotle. "Categories." In *The Complete Works of Aristotle: The Revised Oxford Translation* (1984). Translated by J.L. Ackrill, edited by Jonathan Barnes, 2–27. Princeton, NJ: Princeton University Press, 1991. http://ai-makurdi.org/wp-content/uploads/2020/03/The-Complete-Works-of-Aristotle-The-Revised-Oxford-Translation-by-Aristotle-Jonathan-Barnes-Editor.pdf.

Ayer, A. J. "The Claims of Philosophy." In *The Meaning of Life*, edited by E. Klemke and S. Cahn, 199–202. 3rd ed. New York: Oxford University Press, 2008.

Baggini, Julian. *What's It All About? Philosophy and the Meaning of Life*. Oxford: Oxford University Press, 2005.

Benatar, David. *Better Never to Have Been: The Harm of Coming into Existence*. New York: Oxford University Press, 2006. https://www.docdroid.net/pPhmtci/david-benatar-better-never-to-have-been-pdf.

———. *The Human Predicament: A Candid Guide to Life's Biggest Questions*. New York: Oxford University Press, 2017. https://www.docdroid.net/pIjEbkw/cauliflower-pdf.

Cahn, Steven M. "Meaningless Lives?" *Puzzles & Perplexities: Collected Essays*, 89–91. 2nd ed. Blue Ridge Summit, PA: Lexington, 2007.

Carlyle, Thomas. *History of Friedrich II. of Prussia Called Frederick the Great*. 1 vol. Cambridge: John Wilson & Son, (1884). https://www.scribd.com/document/144935472/Friedrich-II-of-Prussia-Frederick-the-Great-VOL-1-Thomas-Carlyle-1884.

Cartwright, David E. *Schopenhauer: A Biography* (2010). New York: Cambridge University Press, 2013. https://assets.cambridge.org/97811076/26959/frontmatter/9781107626959_frontmatter.pdf.

Chaucer, Geoffrey. *Chaucer's Canterbury Tales* (1894), edited by Alfred Pollard, verses 859–864. 1 vol. New York: MacMillan, 2016.

Chomsky, Noam. *Syntactic Structures* (1957). 2nd ed. New York: Mouton de Gruyter, 2002. https://tallinzen.net/media/readings/chomsky_syntactic_structures.pdf.

Cottingham, John. *On the Meaning of Life* (2003). New York: Routledge, 2005. https://www.vediciluminations.com/downloads/Academic%20General/

Cottingham_John_-_The_Meaning_of_Life_in_Hinduism_and_Buddhism.pdf.

Craig, William Lane. "The Absurdity of Life Without God." *The Meaning of Life.* Edited by E. D. Klemke, 40–56. 2nd ed. New York: Oxford University Press, 2000.

Descartes, René. *Meditations on First Philosophy with Selections from the Objections and Replies.* Translated by Michael Moriarty. New York: Oxford University Press, 2008. https://eclass.uoa.gr/modules/document/file.php/PHS414/Meditations%20on%20First%20Philosophy_%20With%20Selections%20from%20the%20Objections%20and%20Replies.pdf.

Durkin, Philip. "Old English – an Overview." *Oxford English Dictionary* web, 2012. https://www.oed.com/discover/old-english-an-overview/.

———. "Middle English – an Overview." *Oxford English Dictionary* web, 2012. https://www.oed.com/discover/middle-english-an-overview/.

Foreman, A. Z. "Act V Scene 5 of MacBeth ('Life's but a Walking Shadow') Read in Elizabethan Pronunciation," *YouTube*, February 3, 2021, video, 4:13. https://www.youtube.com/watch?v=cuavC5dXCi8.

Gelderen, Elly van. *Analyzing Syntax through texts: Old, Middle, and Early Modern English.* Edinburgh: Edinburgh University Press, 2018.

Goetz, Stewart, and Joshua Seachris. *What is This Thing Called the Meaning of Life?* New York: Routledge, 2020.

Gray, John. *Straw Dogs: Thoughts on Humans and Other Animals* (2002). London: Granta, 2003. https://mlpol.net/images/src/E93780883A08B133 89888E4F3AC44D93-3898982.pdf.

Greenbaum, Sidney. *English Grammar.* New York: Oxford University Press, 1996. https://khmercollection.files.wordpress.com/2011/03/english-grammar.pdf.

Hawking, Stephen, and Leonard Mlodinow. *The Grand Design.* New York: Bantam, 2010.

Hepburn, R. W. "Questions About the Meaning of Life." *Religious Studies* 1 (1966) 125–40. https://www.doi.org/10.1017/S0034412500002419.

Hobbes, Thomas. *Hobbes's Leviathan: Reprinted from the Edition of 1651,* with an essay from W. G. Pogson Smith. London: Oxford University Press, 1965. https://files.libertyfund.org/files/869/0161_Bk.pdf.

Hubbard, Elbert. "William H. Seward." *Little Journeys: To the Homes of American Statesmen.* New York: G. P. Putnam's Sons, 1898. https://archive.org/details/littlejourneyst1858hubb/page/370/mode/2up.

Hume, David. *An Enquiry Concerning Human Understanding.* Chicago: The Open Court, 1900. https://ia800204.us.archive.org/18/items/enquiryconcernino1hume/enquiryconcernino1hume.pdf.

Kant, Immanuel. "Appendix to the Transcendental Dialectic." In *Critique of Pure Reason.* Translated by Norman Kemp Smith, 532–549, London: MacMillan, 1929. http://strangebeautiful.com/other-texts/kant-first-critique-kemp-smith.pdf.

Kekes, John. "The Meaning of Life." *Midwest Studies in Philosophy* 24 (2002) 17–34. https://onlinelibrary.wiley.com/doi/abs/10.1111/1475-4975.00018.

Kierkegaard, Søren. *Fear and Trembling*, Translated by Walter Lowrie. Princeton: Princeton University Press, 1941. https://www.sorenkierkegaard.nl/artikelen/Engels/101.%20Fear%20and%20Trembling%20book%20Kierkegaard.pdf.

Kind, Johann Adam Gottlieb. *Über die Bildung Juristischer Staatsdiener und besonders der Räthe in den Justiz-Collegien* [The Formation of Legal, Civil Servants and, Especially, the Councils in Judicial Colleges]. Leipzig: Göschen, 1818.

Lurie, Yuval. *Wittgenstein on the Human Spirit*. New York: Rodopi, 2012.

Merriam-Webster.com online dictionary, *Merriam-Webster*. https://www.merriam-webster.com/dictionary/life.

Müeller, Friedrich Max. *The Science of Language Founded on Lectures Delivered at the Royal Institution in 1861 and 1863*. 1 vol. New York: Charles Scribner's Sons, 1891.

Nielsen, Kai. "Linguistic Philosophy and 'the Meaning of Life.' " *The Meaning of Life*, edited by E. D. Klemke, 233–56. 2nd ed. New York: Oxford University Press, 2000.

Norvig, Peter. "English Letter Frequency Counts: Mayzner Revisited or ETAOIN SRHLDCU." *Norvig*. https://norvig.com/mayzner.html.

Nozick, Robert. *Philosophical Explanations*. Cambridge, Massachussetts: The Belknap Press of Harvard University Press, 1981. https://www.skepdic.ru/wp-content/uploads/2013/05/Nozick.pdf.

Pearsall, Judy, ed. *The Concise Oxford Dictionary of Current English*. 10th ed. New York: Oxford University Press, 1999.

Phillips, Patrick J. J. *The Challenge of Relativism: Its Nature and Limits*. London: Bloomsbury, 2011.

Plato. "Cratylus." In *Plato: Complete Works*, translated by C. D. C. Reeve, edited by John M. Cooper and D. S. Hutchinson, 101–56. Indianapolis, Indiana: Hackett, 1997.

Rawls, John. *A Theory of Justice* (1971). Cambridge, Massachusetts: The Belknap Press of Harvard University Press, 1999. https://giuseppecapograssi.files.wordpress.com/2014/08/rawls99.pdf.

Schopenhauer, Arthur. *Gesammelte Briefe* [Collected Letters]. Edited by Arthur Hübscher. Bonn: Bouvier, 1978.

———. "On the Sufferings of the World." In *The Essays of Arthur Schopenhauer; Studies in Pessimism*. Edited by Juliet Sutherland *et al.*, translated by T. Bailey Saunders, 2–9. Blackmask Online, 2004. https://www.spiritual-minds.com/philosophy/assorted/Philosophy%20-%20Arthur%20Schopenhauer%20-%20Studies%20In%20Pessimism.pdf.

———. *The World as Will and Representation*. Translated by E. F. J. Payne. 2 vols. New York: Dover, 1966. https://www.antilogicalism.com/wp-content/uploads/2017/07/schopenhauer-the-world-as-will-and-representation-v2.pdf.

Seachris, Joshua. "The Meaning of Life as Narrative: A new Proposal for Interpreting Philosophy's 'Primary' Question." *Philo* 12 (2009) 5–23. https://www.doi.org/10.5840/philo20091211.

———. *Theism, Naturalism, and Narrative: A Linguistic and Metaphysical Proposal on the Meaning of Life.* PhD Diss., Oklahoma University, 2010. https://www.shareok.org/bitstream/handle/11244/319128/Seachris_ou_0169D_10469.pdf?sequence=1&isAllowed=y.

Shakespeare, William. "Macbeth (Folio I, 1623)." *Internet Shakespeare Editions,* edited by Anthony Dawson. University of Victoria. https://internetshakespeare.uvic.ca/doc/Mac_F1/complete/index.html.

Sharpe, Bob. "In Praise of the Meaningless life." *Philosophy Now* 24 (Summer 1999) 15. https://philosophynow.org/issues/24/In_Praise_of_the_Meaningless_Life.

Simpson, J. "The First Dictionaries of English." *Oxford English Dictionary* website, 2012. https://public.oed.com/blog/the-first-dictionaries-of-english/. Note: as of 2023, the entry that was accessed through the given URL disappeared, and its fate is unknown.

Smart, J. J. C., "Meaning and Purpose." *Philosophy Now* 24 (Summer 1999) 16. https://philosophynow.org/issues/24/Meaning_and_Purpose.

Stockwell, Robert. "How Much Shifting Actually Occurred in the Historical English Vowel Shift?" In *Studies in the History of the English Language: A Millennial Perspective,* edited by Donka Minkova and Robert Stockwell, 267–81. New York: Mouton de Gruyter, 2002. https://www.doi.org/10.1515/9783110197143.2.267.

Taylor, Richard. "The Meaning of Life." In *The Meaning of Life,* edited by E. D. Klemke, 167–75. 2nd ed. New York: Oxford University Press, 2000.

Tchertkoff, Vladimir. *The Last Days of Tolstoy.* Translated by Natalie A. Duddington. London: William Heinemann, 1922. https://www.openlibrary.org/books/OL6656141M/The_last_days_of_Tolstoy.

"When to use Definite vs. Indefinite Articles." *Thesaurus,* February 12, 2017. https://www.thesaurus.com/e/grammar/definite-vs-indefinite-articles/.

Tolstoy, Leo. *Confession.* Translated by David Patterson. New York: W. W. Norton & Company, 1983. https://www.arvindguptatoys.com/arvindgupta/confessions-tolstoy.pdf.

Wainwright, Oliver. "In Iceland, 'Respect the Elves – or Else.'" *The Guardian.* March 25, 2015. https://www.theguardian.com/artanddesign/2015/mar/25/iceland-construction-respect-elves-or-else.

Warren, Rich. "More Than Half of Iceland Believes in Elves." *National Geographic.* December 1, 2017. https://www.nationalgeographic.com/travel/article/believes-elves-exist-mythology#:~:text=Yes%2C%20elves.,say%20it's%20possible%20they%20exist.

Wilson, Edward O. *Consilience: the Unity of Knowledge* (1998). 1st ed. New York: Vintage, April 1999. https://www.wtf.tw/ref/wilson.pdf.

Wolf, Susan. "Happiness and Meaning: Two Aspects of the Good Life." *Social Philosophy and Policy* 14 (1997) 207–25, https://www.doi.org/10.1017/s0265052500001734.

———. "Meaning in Life and Why it Matters: Lectures I & II." Transcript, 7–8. Presented at *The Tanner Lectures on Human Values*, Princeton University, NJ, November 2007. https://www.tannerlectures.utah.edu/_resources/documents/a-to-z/w/Wolf_07.pdf.

"Search Omni Catalogue." *York University Libraries*, https://www.library.yorku.ca/web/.

Index